PEOPLE ARE SAYING

"Finally an introduction to Jung's thought that I can recommend to students and colleagues alike! Here is a broad ranging and sensitive text that does not propagate Newtonian misconceptions, but does full justice to both the archaic and postmodern aspects of Jung's mind. In the bargain, it is probably the most readable introduction on the market."
—Allan Combs, author of *Synchronicity*

"Robertson has done a tremendous service to anyone who would wish to understand Jung, his theory, its significance for one's personal life and for our time. Robertson has done his homework on Jung."
—Henry Reed, *Venture Inward*

"If there is any book that could bring a comprehension of Jung to the academic world, this is it. It simply belongs in the library of every literate person who is on a path of evolving consciousness."
—Ernest Lawrence Rossi, *Psychological Perspectives*

"This book is very different from the usual kind of introductory work on Jung, because of its relaxed and characteristically clear discussions of the ideas and theories of Jung. I was especially struck by the refreshing dearth of technical language that is so often found in Jungian studies material. Robertson's writing makes one want to read Jung. I would recommend this work to teachers who want to introduce students to Jung and to anyone who is just curious."
—Gail Duke, *Artifex*

"This book is a preliminary excursion into the Jungian universe, and worth the time."
—Les Stern, *Fate Magazine* 1993

". . . Dr. Robertson is able to put high-order theory into simple, elegant, comprehensible prose. Without 'popularizing' theory, he makes theory easy to understand. He is not only good at this; he is genuinely gifted."
—Dr. Michael Washburn, *S.U.N.Y. Press* 1992

On The Hudson

Jung

BOOK SERIES

The Jung on the Hudson Book Series was instituted by The New York Center for Jungian Studies in 1997. This ongoing series is designed to present books that will be of interest to individuals of all fields, as well as mental health professionals, who are interested in exploring the relevance of the psychology and ideas of C. G. Jung to their personal lives and professional activities.

For more information about the annual Jung on the Hudson seminars, this series, and the New York Center for Jungian Studies contact: Aryeh Maidenbaum, Ph.D., 27 North Chestnut St., Suite 3, New Paltz, NY 12561, telephone (845) 256-0191, fax (845) 256-0196.

For more information about becoming part of this series, contact: Nicolas-Hays, Inc., P. O. Box 1126, Berwick, ME 03901-1126, telephone: (207) 698-1041, fax: (207) 698-1042, e-mail: info@nicolashays.com.

Beginner's Guide to
JUNGIAN
PSYCHOLOGY

Robin Robertson

NICOLAS-HAYS, INC.
Berwick, Maine

First published in 1992 by
Nicolas-Hays, Inc.
P.O. Box 540206
Lake Worth, Florida 33454-0206
www.nicolashays.com

Distributed to the trade by
Red Wheel/Weiser, LLC
Box 612
York Beach, ME 03910
www.redwheelweiser.com

Copyright © 1992 Robin Robertson

Library of Congress Cataloging-in-Publication Data

Robertson, Robin.
    Beginner's guide to Jungian psychology / by Robin Robertson.
      p. cm.
    Includes bibliographical references and index.
    1. Psychoanalysis. 2. Jung, C. G. (Carl Gustav), 1875–1961.
    I. Title.
    BF173.R5515   1992
    150.19'54—dc20   92–1772

ISBN-13: 978-0-89254-022-8   CIP
ISBN-10: 0-89254-022-2

VG

Cover art copyright ©1992 Rob Schouten. Used by kind permission.
Typeset in 11 point Palatino

Printed in the United States of America

10 09 08 07
12 11 10 9 8 7

TABLE OF CONTENTS

ILLUSTRATIONS

ACKNOWLEDGMENTS

To Ernest Lawrence Rossi, whose appreciation for my early work made me realize that my somewhat idiosyncratic insights into Jungian psychology could be of worth to others. In those early days, Ernie often understood what I was trying to say before I did myself. His own conviction that there was no dichotomy between the scientific and spiritual aspects of Jung's work helped bolster my own similar conviction. Without his enthusiasm, support and intellectual challenge, I doubt that I would have had the courage to find my own voice.

I would also like to acknowledge the help that both Richard Messer and James Hollis provided in carefully reviewing and suggesting changes to early versions of this book. Without their friendly criticism, this would have been a much poorer product.

In addition, I would like to credit the following sources for quoted material that appears at the beginning of each chapter:

Carl Jung, *The Collected Works of C. G. Jung*, trans. R. F. C. Hull, Bollingen Series XX (Princeton: Princeton University Press):

Vol. 8: *The Structure and Dynamics of the Psyche*, copyright © 1960, 1969, 111.

Vol. 18: *The Symbolic Life*, copyright © 1980, 13.

Vol. 18: 14.

Vol. 6: *Psychological Types*, copyright © 1971, 558.

Vol. 17: *The Development of Personality,* copyright © 1954, 331b.

Vol. 17: 338.

Robin Robertson, *C. G. Jung and the Archetypes of the Collective Unconscious* (New York: Peter Lang, 1987), p. 138.

The following sources were used for the illustrations that appear in this book: *Dore's Spot Illustrations,* selected by C. B. Grafton, Dover Pictorial Archive Series, New York: Dover Publications, 1987, figures 1, 10, 20; *Magic, Supernaturalism and Religion,* by Kurt Seligman, New York: Pantheon Books, 1948, figure 2; *Witchcraft, Magic & Alchemy,* by Grillot de Givry, New York: Dover Publications, 1971, figure 4; *1001 Spot Illustrations of the Lively Twenties,* ed. C. B. Grafton, New York: Dover Pictorial Archive Series, Dover Publications, 1986, figures 9, 12, 15; *William Morris: Ornamentation & Illustrations from the Kelmscott Chaucer,* New York: Dover Pictorial Archive Series, Dover Publications, 1973, figure 11; *Pictorial Archive of Decorative Renaissance Woodcuts,* ed. Jost Amman, New York: Dover Pictorial Archive Series, Dover Publications, 1968, figures 13, 14, 16; *Humorous Victorian Spot Illustrations,* ed. C. B. Grafton, New York: Dover Pictorial Archive Series, Dover Publications, 1985, figure 17.

CHAPTER 1

JUNG AND THE UNCONSCIOUS

Every advance in culture is, psychologically, an exten-sion of consciousness, a coming to consciousness that can take place only through discrimination.

—*Carl Jung*

This book is about the psychology discovered by Carl Gustav Jung in the first half of the 20th century and its relevance for all of us as we pass into the new world of the 21st century. Jung was a truly original thinker whose ideas are still largely unknown or misunderstood. He wasn't always right; pioneers never are. His view of reality was so different from the prevailing world view that it has often been difficult for fellow psychologists and scientists to grasp what he actually meant.

This wasn't helped by a writing style that was both too literary for his academic colleagues and too scholarly for his literary admirers. Artists and writers have fought their way through to an understanding of the essence of Jung better than the academicians, but they have often generalized too quickly, unable to cope with the breadth and depth of Jung's mind.

In this book, I will try to present a unified picture of Jung's thought, perhaps more unified than is found in his collected writings, but one which I think is a fair presentation of his ideas. My emphasis will be on the practical utility of his ideas, since he has so often been dismissed as impractical and unrealistic. But first, I want to present some idea of the kind of man Jung was, how and why he came to develop the most original world view of the 20th century.

JUNG AND FREUD

Like Sigmund Freud, his still more famous mentor, Jung was a medical doctor who became one of the early pioneers in the new field of psychoanalysis. Though a clinical psychologist, Jung also did pioneering work in experimental psychology that later led to the lie detector (whose misuse Jung would have abhorred). However, Jung first attracted the attention of Sigmund Freud with his early concept of a *complex* (i.e., feelings, images and memories so clustered about a single concept, such as "the mother," that they form a whole in the mind). Complexes will be discussed at some length in chapter 2. Freud was nineteen years older than Jung and had already done some of his greatest work. Psychoanalysis was as yet nearly unknown and Freud was either dismissed or reviled by both the medical and academic communities.

You couldn't describe a more perfect situation for Jung to hero-worship Freud, nor for Freud to "adopt" a chosen disciple. In 1906, Jung met Freud and soon after became first Freud's favorite colleague, then his appointed successor. Unfortunately for Freud's plans, Jung was not cut out to be anyone's disciple. Freud and Jung were very different types of men who saw the world in very different ways (as we will see when we discuss Jung's theory of psychological types in chapter 4).

Freud was 50 and felt he had already discovered the essential ideas that described the structure and dynamics of the human *psyche*. (*Psyche* is the word that Jung used to describe the totality of all our psychological processes. It seems a better choice than either brain or mind, since it doesn't limit itself to, or separate itself from, the physical.) Freud wanted followers who would take his ideas and develop their consequences. While Jung admired Freud, and thought many of his ideas were useful, he believed the human psyche was far more complex than Freud proposed. While Freud's theories hardened into dogma, Jung pursued his own work with his patients wherever it took him. And it took him places that didn't fit into Freud's theory.

SYMBOLS OF TRANSFORMATION

For example, Freud's concept of the Oedipus complex deeply impressed Jung, but Jung saw something different than Freud intended. In brief, Freud argued that the taboo against incest lies deep inside each of us. Because it is ubiquitous, it invariably had to find expression in our myths and literature; Freud felt that it had found its perfect expression in the myth of Oedipus, who unwittingly killed his father Laius and married his mother Jocasta. When Oedipus and Jocasta finally discovered the truth, Jocasta committed suicide and Oedipus blinded himself. Freud argues that this conflict is primal, that it is repeated over and over in all of our lives, especially in the lives of boys between the ages of 4 and 5. At that age (according to Freud), they love their mothers intensely and hate their fathers.

Freud made the Oedipal complex the cornerstone of his theory; it was the single most significant psychic element that underlay masculine development. Jung saw something much more exciting in Freud's discovery: the idea that all the ancient myths still lived inside each of us. In the story of Oedipus, while Freud found a description for all psychic development, Jung saw a single example of a multitude of psychic invariants inside each of us.

Fabled Greek mathematician Archimedes was that rarest of men: a theoretician who could turn his theories to practical use. He used mathematical relationships to develop ingenious combinations of pulleys and levers, which he used to move enormous objects. There is an apocryphal story that, flushed with his success, Archimedes cried, "Give me a place to stand on and I will move the earth!"

Like Archimedes, Jung realized that Freud had discovered a single example of how psychology could escape from personal history by turning to the history of the race as it was recorded in mythology. This historical approach provided both a place to stand on that was outside the patient and a lever to move the patient's psyche. Jung immediately began to pursue this exciting new direction in psychology.

In 1912, Jung published the first fruits of his research as *Transformations and Symbols of the Libido* (later extensively rewritten and published as *Symbols of Transformation* in 1952). This book proposed the heretical notion that libido was not merely sexual energy, but psychic energy, and that an image in a dream was much more than a simple rebus that could be decoded to reveal a forbidden sexual desire. In a dazzling display of scholarly detective work, Jung turned to the whole field of mythology for amplification of the fantasies of a single woman in the incipient stages of schizophrenia. (The woman, referred to as "Miss Frank Miller," was a patient of Theodore Flournoy, who had published her fantasies in 1906.)

Where Freud "reduced" fantasy and dream images to a single mythological reference (the Oedipus complex), Jung "amplified" the images in her fantasies by showing parallels throughout the varied mythologies of many cultures and ages. As the fantasies unfolded, he was able to show a pattern emerging that led ineluctably toward a split of the psyche—schizophrenia.

How could the images in a modern woman's fantasies repeat themes from myths thousands of years old, myths which the woman had never read? Our modern world view sees each of us as a blank slate, upon which experience writes its stories. Perhaps it was all in Jung's imagination. Perhaps his analysis was a clever fiction. Was Jung correct in relating her fantasies to mythological patterns which he could interpret as the various stages leading to schizophrenia?

Well, yes he was correct. When, sometime later, Jung discussed his conclusions with Flournoy, Flournoy confirmed that the course of the woman's illness closely matched the pattern Jung described. It's hard to explain how this could occur unless there is a collective underpinning to the psyche, which supplies the images of myths, dreams, and fantasies.

This was too much for Freud, and he soon broke off relations with Jung. Freudians have usually taken Freud's side in presenting this break, Jungians take Jung's side. But it was probably inevitable they would have to split, for they saw the world through different lenses. Like many another father and son (for so Freud and Jung were in essence), Freud felt betrayed by Jung, Jung felt abandoned by Freud. There is some validity to both their views. With his insistence on a total independence from convention, Jung would have been a difficult son for any father to tolerate. With his strong (and sometimes rigid) views about the nature of the psyche, Freud was an impossible father for any son to tolerate. (Virtually all of his psychoanalytic "sons" left him one after another, beginning with Adler.)

But understandable or not, it was a bitter pill for Jung to swallow. For the rest of his life, Jung was forced to follow a solitary path in his exploration of this collective bedrock that underlies individual consciousness. The book you are about to read is about Carl Jung's discovery and exploration of the "unconscious as an objective and collective psyche," which he was later to refer to simply as the "collective unconscious." He called it "collective" because it consists of images and behavioral patterns not acquired by an individual in his or her lifetime, yet accessible to all individuals in all times; "unconscious" because it can't be reached through conscious awareness.

MYTHS IN OUR LIVES

Scientists and academics have always scoffed at the concept of a collective unconscious. They "know" that it is impossible for people to have any memories that weren't acquired in this lifetime. It seems a very odd notion for those of us raised in these supposedly rational times. At a time when we thrash about in a vain search for absent spiritual values, we pretend that the spirit can be reduced to the mind. At a time when we live increasingly in our minds, cut off from the natural world around us, we pretend that the mind can in turn be reduced to the brain. We are positive that there is a material explanation for everything. Any other description of reality is dismissed as primitive superstition.

Yet because of this materialism, we live isolated and alienated from one another. Loneliness and despair have become the normal condition in our advanced Western civilization. Locked within ourselves, we desperately yearn for some sense of relatedness—to our jobs, to our religion, to another person, to the world around us, to ourselves.

Jung's psychology offers a way out of this cul-de-sac. It's not a total answer, but it presents a possibility for a new way of viewing the world. In contrast to the cold, impersonal mechanistic world of materialism, Jung describes a warm, personal, organic world in which each person is connected to each and every other person, where each is connected to every aspect of the universe. Yet each person is also a unique individual with a unique destiny which he calls *individuation* (i.e., the developmental path that each of us takes during his or her lifetime).

Like any such total view, Jung's picture of reality leaves a number of unanswered questions. The concept of a collective unconscious opens many doors that had previously been closed to Western thought. Traditionally, psychology (along with 20th-century philosophy and science) has dealt with such troublesome questions by limiting itself to those questions that it can answer. Any other questions, especially metaphysical questions, are regarded as nonsense (literally "non" sense, not relatable to sensory description). Unfortunately (or fortunately, in my view) the world is more complex than our systems of thought. Jung's psychology honors all the complexity that each of us experiences in the world. If he is not able to answer all the questions, at least he doesn't deny that the questions exist.

Jung's concept of the collective unconscious is neither a philosophic construct nor a religious dogma; it is an attempt, albeit sometimes a rather primitive attempt, to present an accurate description of the inner world of the psyche and its relationship with the outer material world. He found this world by carefully exploring the dreams of his patients, then relating them to similar themes he found in the fairy tales, mythology, art, and culture of the entire world.

This wasn't an academic exercise; he turned to mythology because it helped him understand and cure patients with real problems. For example, he might find a symbol in a patient's dream that puzzled him. He looked in mythology and found a myth where the symbol had occurred before. Since myths tell stories about human conflicts, Jung could understand the conflict that the patient was experiencing, a conflict that the patient had kept hidden from himself and from Jung. If dreams are meaningless, it should have just been chance that the dream repeated an image from mythology. The conflict reflected in the myth should have had little if anything to do with the patient's actual problem. But it did. Time and again, it did (and still does).

We don't need faith to accept Jung's view of reality; all we need is the courage to honestly explore our own inner world as Jung himself did. This exploration is made easier because Jung has already explored it himself and provided a map of the territory. We don't have to accept his map on faith. He always asked that we approach the psyche as if we know nothing about it. Yet, if we carefully observe what we encounter in our inner life, we will find that our observations fit closely into Jung's model. That's because there actually is a collective unconscious; it's not just a theory.

When we peel away everything that is personal in the psyche, something still remains, something common to all men and women in all times and cultures. Because it is literally unconscious, we can't experience it directly. Like particle physicists observing the tracks left by subatomic particles in a bubble chamber, we have to observe the unconscious through the tracks it leaves in our dreams and fantasies. But we can construct models based on those observations, models that describe (note that they describe, not explain) both its structure and its dynamic relationship with consciousness.

Before embarking on that journey, we need to know something about this remarkable man—C. G. Jung—so that we can better understand how he was able to make his unique discoveries.

TIES TO NATURE

Carl Jung was born in Kesswil, a rural region of Switzerland, in 1875. His father was a minister who moved the family to a new parish when Carl was 6 months old and again when he was 4 years old. Both parishes were in rural settings (though the latter parish was near the city of Basel). Jung was a lonely child with no siblings or playmates until he began school (a younger sister was born when he was 9). Cut off from the companionship of other children, he was forced both inward upon his own resources and outward toward the beauty of the natural world around him. Though his later life was filled with deep and significant loves and friendships, he was always to remain a loner who believed strongly that knowledge should ultimately be rooted in direct observation.

In Jung's time, the rural Swiss still lived in a world of mountains and lakes, forests and fields, that hadn't changed significantly in hundreds of years. The Swiss have had a policy of political neutrality since 1515, desiring only peace and stability (though that balance was upset during Napoleon's reign). As a people they have a stolid, earthy quality, rooted in the natural abundance that surrounds them. It's important to recognize this earthy

Swiss quality in Jung, since so many have dismissed his description of the psyche as fantasy.[1]

Nature was to provide a source of comfort and nourishment for the rest of Jung's life. As an adult, soon after his marriage in 1903, he built the home he would live in the rest of his life, in Kussnacht, on the shore of Lake Zurich. In 1923, after the death of his mother, he also built a stone tower nearby in Bollingen. From then until his death in 1961, he was to divide his time between living with his family in Kussnacht and living in primitive isolation in his tower in Bollingen. He made additions to the tower in 1927, 1931, 1935, and a final addition shortly after his wife's death in 1955. He learned how to quarry and carve stone in order to do much of the building work on the tower himself. Jung movingly describes his relationship to the tower and to nature in his spiritual autobiography, *Memories, Dreams, Reflections*.

> At Bollingen I am in the midst of my true life, I am most deeply myself. . . . At times I feel as if I am spread out over the landscape and inside things, and am myself living in every tree, in the splashing of the waves, in the clouds and the animals that come and go, in the procession of the season. There is nothing in the Tower that has not grown into its own form over the decades, nothing with which I am not linked. Here everything has its

---

[1]Jung's willingness to attribute characteristics to nations and races has aroused the ire of many critics. They confuse such honest observation with prejudice. But don't we all know that different cultures have different traits? The Germans and the French have struggled throughout history as much because of the difference in their perception of the world as because of their struggles over territory. To say that a nation has certain characteristics isn't to insist that everyone has them, nor to take away anyone's individuality. Acknowledging that different nations have different personalities is no different than acknowledging that different individuals have different personalities.

history, and mine; here is space for the spaceless kingdom of the world's and the psyche's hinterland.[2]

HIDDEN FORCES

Unlike city dwellers, people who live in rural areas recognize that the world is filled with unseen forces. Those who live close to nature, watching the annual cycles of birth, death and rebirth, know the power hidden beneath the seemingly commonplace. As Wordsworth describes this feeling in "Tintern Abbey,"

> . . . A sense sublime
> Of something far more deeply interfused,
> Whose dwelling is the light of setting suns,
> And the round ocean and the living air,
> And the blue sky, and in the mind of man:
> A motion and a spirit, that impels
> All thinking things, all objects of all thought,
> And rolls through all things.[3]

That was also Jung's world. In contrast, Jung's father was the sort of minister who was never able to live in peace with that hidden spiritual realm. His religion was dry and desiccated because he never believed in his own vocation. Jung wasn't to find a fitting father until as a young man he met Freud. Jung turned instead to his mother for spiritual support. She introduced Jung to Goethe and his eternal story of the temptation of Faust by the demon Mephistopheles. This story of the knowledge

---

[2]C. G. Jung, *Memories, Dreams, Reflections* (New York: Pantheon Books, 1973, revised edition), pp. 225–226.
[3]Jack Stillinger, ed., *William Wordsworth: Selected Poems and Prefaces* (Boston: Houghton Mifflin Company, 1965), p. 110.

and power hidden within, and the moral conflicts caused by that knowledge and power, was to fascinate Jung throughout his life.

Later, as a young college student, Jung methodically read all that he could of psychic phenomena. Jung's attitude toward these phenomena was typical of his attitude toward other such supposedly irrational, superstitious matters throughout his life. He neither accepted the explanations he read blindly nor condemned them out of hand. Instead he was fascinated by these strange events and attempted to discuss them with his friends. They dismissed the topics, but Jung sensed that their derision concealed anxiety. He wondered why his friends were so sure that such things were impossible. And, budding psychologist that he was, he wondered at least as much why they had so much anxiety in approaching the subject.

In 1902, he wrote his first scientific paper about a series of seances he attended. They were conducted by a young woman (who also happened to be his cousin) who gained local fame for a time as a medium. Jung was fascinated to find that occasionally the messages communicated in trance possessed an authority and intelligence greater than the girl seemed to possess out of trance. This wasn't always so: sometimes the messages were simply pastiches of information gleaned by his cousin in her daily life and readings. But it was that other voice of authority that interested Jung.

PERSONALITY NUMBER 1 AND NUMBER 2

Jung had earlier personal experiences with the power hidden inside the psyche. When he was 12, and a friend's father scolded him for disobedience, Jung reacted with an unusual fury. He couldn't believe the audacity of the man, daring to criticize someone as important as Jung felt himself to be. At that moment, Jung felt that he was an old man of power and means, someone to be respected and obeyed. Almost before the thought was in his mind, he was struck by the ludicrous contrast between that old, dignified man and the schoolboy who actually stood before his friend's father. How to reconcile the two disparate images?

He came to realize that he contained two different personalities: the young schoolboy the world saw, and a powerful older man who had seen and done many things the young schoolboy had yet to experience. This older personality was quite specific: Jung visualized him as an elderly 18th-century gentleman of wealth and position, complete with "buckled shoes and a white wig."

Jung continued to experience this "other," who he termed personality No. 2 (in contrast to his normal personality No. 1) throughout his life. Even as a young boy, he realized this was a positive part of his psyche, not something to be feared as an indication that he was crazy. Many people in similar circumstances would have viewed No. 2 as proof of reincarnation, proof that they were experiencing a prior life. Jung never thought of No. 2 in those terms. Rather, No. 2 seemed to Jung to be a personification of another half of his personality which was normally hidden from consciousness. He later came to term that hidden half the *collective unconscious*.

Earlier yet, Jung had encountered this twin personality in his mother. Normally a kindly, conventional fat woman, infrequently he would have glimpses of another personality, one with infinitely more knowledge and authority. This No. 2 personality of his mother's often appeared at night, a strange personality more seeress than mother. Jung was both fascinated and frightened by this side of his mother, a pair of emotions he was later to realize characterized all dealings with the collective unconscious.

So there we have most of the essential background that was to lead Jung to the discovery and exploration of the collective unconscious: 1) the lonely seeker after truth; 2) the lifelong devotion to nature itself in preference to theories about nature; 3) the refusal to dismiss unusual experiences on rationalistic grounds; 4) the experience in himself, his cousin and his mother of the incredibly greater knowledge and authority of personality No. 2.

Throughout his career, Jung described what he encountered in the psyche in preference to explaining it. Like many another scientist, and Jung was in large part a scientist, Jung developed "models" in order to provide a structure for the psychic facts he was cataloging. However, he always viewed his models as provisional and always searched for still better models. The next chapter will describe one of Jung's models for the basic structure of the psyche, and illustrate some of the complexity of the relationship between consciousness and the unconscious. In later chapters we will discuss Jung's view of dreams, his model of psychological types, and then his principal model for the process of individuation.

CHAPTER 2

THE PSYCHE

The conscious mind moreover is characterized by a certain narrowness. It can hold only a few simultaneous contents at a given moment. All the rest is unconscious at the time, and we only get a sort of continuation or a general understanding or awareness of a conscious world through the succession of conscious moments. We can never hold an image of totality because our consciousness is too narrow. . . . The area of the unconscious is enormous and always continuous, while the area of consciousness is a restricted field of momentary vision.

—Carl Jung

According to Jung, consciousness, seemingly the *sine qua non* of humanity, is just the tip of the iceberg. Beneath consciousness lies a much larger substratum of forgotten or repressed personal memories, feelings, and behaviors, which Jung termed the personal unconscious. And beneath that lies the deep sea of the collective unconscious, huge and ancient, filled with all the images and behaviors that have been repeated over and over through-out the history of not only mankind, but life itself. As Jung said: ". . . the deeper you go, the broader the base becomes."[1]

If Jung's model seems a little hard to accept, remember that even modern men and women live very little of their lives consciously. Our distant ancestors managed to live and die with even less individual consciousness. If our closest modern cousins—the chimpanzees and great apes—are representative of our hominid ancestors, they had some degree of self-awareness, but certainly much less than we do. As we proceed backward in evolutionary development, to animals less developed than chimps and apes and hominids, the degree of consciousness becomes so attenuated that it is difficult to still think of it as con-sciousness. Is an amoeba conscious?

The 19th-century German biologist and philosopher Ernst Haekel argued that "ontogeny recapitulates phylog-eny," i.e., that an individual's development goes through the same stages as the evolutionary development of the species.[2] Though Haekel's wonderful catch phrase is somewhat overstated, it is nevertheless true that each of us carries much of the record of our evolutionary history within the structure of our bodies. Our alimentary tract functions much like the tubular creatures which swam in the primeval oceans over half a billion years ago; like our alimentary tract, they were little more than a tube through which nutrients could pass and be absorbed for use as food. The most elementary part of our brain—the spinal cord, hindbrain and midbrain (which scientist Paul

---

[1]Carl Jung, *The Collected Works of C. G. Jung*, trans. R. F. C. Hull, Bol-lingen Series XX. Vol. 5: *Symbols of Transformation*, copyright © 1956 (Princeton: Princeton University Press), p. xxv. All subsequent refer-ences to Jung's *Collected Works* will be to this translation and series.
[2]W. L. Reese, *Dictionary of Philosophy and Religion* (Atlantic Highlands, NJ: Humanities Press, 1980), p. 206.

MacLean calls the "neural chassis")—wouldn't have been out of place in fish swimming the oceans four hundred million years ago.

In *The Dragons of Eden*,[3] Carl Sagan popularized MacLean's triune brain model, which presents the brain that surrounds the neural chassis as three separate brains, each piled on top of the other, each representing a stage of evolution. Proceeding from the oldest to the most recent, these three brains might be characterized as follows:

1) the R-complex, or *reptile brain*, which "plays an important role in aggressive behavior, territoriality, ritual and the establishment of social hierarchies."[4] The R-complex probably appeared with the first reptiles about a quarter of a billion years ago;

2) the limbic system (which includes the pituitary gland), or *mammal brain*, which largely controls our emotions. It "governs social awareness and relationships—belonging, caring, empathy, compassion and group preservation."[5] It probably appeared not more than a hundred and fifty million years ago; and finally—

3) the neocortex, the *primate brain*, "is more oriented than the others to external stimuli."[6] It controls the higher brain functions, such as reasoning, deliberation and language. The neocortex also controls complex perceptual tasks, especially the

---

[3]Carl Sagan, *The Dragons of Eden: Speculations of the Evolution of Human Intelligence* (New York: Ballantine Books, 1977).
[4]Sagan, *The Dragons of Eden*, p. 63.
[5]"Gray's Theory Incorporates Earlier Evolutionary Model of 'Triune Brain,'" *Brain/Mind Bulletin* (March 29, 1982), p. 4.
[6]"Gray's Theory," p. 4.

control of vision. In fact, though no single acronym accurately describes its complexity, terming the neocortex the "visual brain" isn't that far removed from accuracy. Though it probably appeared in the higher mammals "several tens of millions of years ago . . . its development accelerated greatly a few million years ago when humans emerged."[7]

The periods of time over which each of these three brains reigned supreme can equally well be regarded as stages of the development of consciousness. The relative lengths of time since each developed corresponds roughly to the amount of control each has over our lives (though I'm stretching the point a bit here). Thus far and away the most vital regulator of human life is the neural chassis, which directs the autonomous functions of our body.

I doubt that we would think of those functions as in any way conscious. Yet whole classes of living creatures still live and die who are no more developed than our neural chassis—insects, mollusks, fish, etc. Is there any sense in which they are conscious? Perhaps so. For example, the awareness of pain is a consciousness of sorts, and one has to go very far down the evolutionary path before all awareness of pain vanishes. Or take a very low level of consciousness: even the amoeba has to recognize the difference between the food it eats and the enemies it flees from in order to survive. Though that recognition may be totally instinctive, those two situations still present the amoeba with different inner experiences. And such differences in inner experience are the beginnings of consciousness.

---

[7]Sagan, *The Dragons of Eden*, p. 58.

CONSCIOUSNESS AND THE TRIUNE BRAIN

It is when we pass on to the oldest of MacLean's three evolutionary brains—the reptile brain—that we start to encounter inner behavior more characteristic of consciousness. However, reptile consciousness is still far removed from what we normally think of as human consciousness. Because reptile consciousness has no element of emotion, we quite rightly associate it with an amorality that repulses us. Reptiles are quite literally cold-blooded, a term we use to refer to a person with no emotional warmth. Yet much of our lives are still governed by the reptile brain; e.g., it is our reptilian brain that drives us to protect and extend our "territory," a concept that has become generalized in humans far beyond physical territory.

While we might be unconscious of the underlying dynamic of our actions when driven by the reptile brain, we are conscious within the parameters set by this brain. When the reptile brain is in control, we are largely driven by deep and ancient instincts, but they are instincts over which we have some degree of control, at least enough control to adapt them to our environment.

The most famous presentation of the reptilian level of consciousness in the Western world is the story of Eve and the serpent in the Bible. The serpent convinces Eve to eat the fruit of the tree of knowledge of good and evil. Before eating the fruit, Adam and Eve live like other animals, content in Paradise. After eating the fruit, Adam and Eve's first reaction is shame at their nakedness. God expels them from Paradise. In other words, as long as men and women are unconscious (as the Bible regards the animals), they are in Paradise. As soon as they become conscious, shame enters the picture and Paradise is gone. And this new consciousness is represented by the serpent—the reptile brain.

Figure 1. Snakes appear in our dreams when we are breaking through to a new level of perception, because our highest spiritual understanding is rooted in our deepest instinctual drives. (*Serpent,* from *Fables of La Fontaine.* Reprinted from *Dore's Spot Illustrations.*)

Egyptian mythology tells another story of the birth of the reptile level of consciousness. The god of creation, Ra (with traits much like Jehovah) had grown old and feeble. His daughter, Isis, couldn't create life herself, so she formed a snake from the dirt at her feet and left it in Ra's path. When Ra's spittle fell on the snake, it came to life and bit Ra on the ankle. Since he hadn't created anything that could injure him this way, he didn't know what to do. He grew sicker and sicker. Isis said she couldn't cure him unless he told her his secret name, which contained his power. Finally, in desperation, Ra gave Isis his name. Though she used it to cure him, she also passed on the power to her husband/brother Osiris. The age of Ra gave way to the age of Osiris.

> . . . every step towards greater consciousness is a kind of Promethean guilt: through knowledge, the gods are as it were robbed of their fire, that is, something that was the property of the uncon-

Figure 2. The Egyptian goddess Isis is often a symbol for initiation into hidden mysteries, because Isis forced Ra to reveal his hidden name—thus bringing about the end of the Age of Ra and the beginning of the Age of Osiris. (*Isis*, from *Oedipus Aegyptiacus*, by Athanasius Kircher, 1652.)

scious powers is torn out of its natural context and subordinated to the whims of the conscious mind.[8]

Interestingly, snakes still appear in our dreams when we are breaking through to a new awareness, which is still so far removed from our normal consciousness that it chills us with its cold-bloodedness. Any such new awareness expels us from our previous "Paradise" of unconsciousness.

When the limbic system takes over and emotion enters the picture, we part company with the reptiles (except for their modern cousins—the birds—who, though descended from the dinosaurs, possess elementary emotions). Mammalian consciousness is quite familiar to us; in fact, social animals that we are, we live a great deal more of our "conscious" life under the control of mammalian consciousness than we do within the primate consciousness determined by the neocortex. As a species, we have had so much longer to adapt to the control of the limbic system, that we feel quite at home when it is in charge. Without the limbic system, we would have no families, tribes, or social groups of any kind; sex would never have developed into love; curiosity would never have passed over into religious awe.

With the appearance of the neocortex, the primate brain, the development of consciousness begins to accelerate. Then once humans appear, biological evolution gives way to cultural evolution. If that were our task, we could follow the increasingly better understood history of our development—from hominids wandering the savannahs of Northern Africa, to tribes of hunter-gatherers, to agricultural humankind, onward to modern humanity. But

---

[8]Carl Jung, *The Collected Works*, Vol. 7: *Two Essays on Analytical Psychology*, copyright © 1953, © 1966 (Princeton: Princeton University Press), 243n.

that's not germane to our discussion of Jung's concept of levels of the unconscious. The significant fact is that even physical science demonstrates that we still contain a history of our evolutionary heritage without the body as a whole, and equally within our neurological structure. Jung's concept of the collective unconscious is an acknowledgment that ancestral history still has a major effect on our lives.

We have no trouble at all accepting that a spider already knows how to spin a web at birth, or that many varieties of fish and birds and turtles don't have to be taught how to find the distant places where they will go to mate. We have more trouble accepting that we humans also carry such a rich instinctual heritage within ourselves. Yet it would be strange indeed if our mammalian brain didn't tell us much that we have to learn about love and sex, if our reptile brain didn't drive us to stake out our own territory in life.

CONSCIOUS AND UNCONSCIOUS

Jung's concept of the levels of the unconscious seems less radical than what we have just discussed. Perhaps Jung might have chosen a better term than unconscious; as we have seen, we are really talking about an increasingly attenuated level of consciousness as we proceed backward in time. There is really no clear demarcation between stages of consciousness. But Jung was writing at an especially species-arrogant point in time, when we were enamored with the successes achieved with the conscious intellect, and Jung wanted to stress that there were other factors at work in our lives.

In their work as clinical psychologists, Freud and Jung were forced to deal with the forces that underlay consciousness. Their patients exhibited symptoms that reflected a conflict between conscious values (which represented the values of family and culture), and instinctual desires (of which they had no conscious awareness). Freud centered exclusively on the sexual instinct, while Jung realized that we each contain a myriad of ancient behaviors and images. Accordingly, Jung chose to split conscious from unconscious at a very advanced point of development—the point at which we become aware of our own inner processes.

In Jung's terms, it is difficult to imagine any non-human animal (with the possible exception of chimps, great apes and dolphins) as conscious. In fact, in that restricted sense of the word, consciousness has only itself developed very recently, and still controls a relatively small part of our lives.

MARSHALL McLUHAN
AND MASS CONSCIOUSNESS

If, for instance, I determine the weight of each stone in a bed of pebbles and get an average weight of five ounces, this tells me very little about the real nature of the pebbles. Anyone who thought, on the basis of these findings, that he could pick up a pebble of five ounces at the first try would be in for a serious disappointment. Indeed, it might well happen that however long he searched he would not find a single pebble weighing exactly five ounces.[9]

---

[9]Carl Jung, *The Collected Works*, Vol. 10: *Civilization in Transition*, copyright © 1964, 1970 (Princeton: Princeton University Press), 493.

Jung was a scientist who believed in objective evidence. However, he felt strongly that the attempt to make psychology a statistical science was misguided. Statistical theories describe the average person, the mass man or woman, not the individual. That sort of statistical knowledge may be useful in physics, but it should have little or no place in psychology. For Jung, a growth in consciousness is always a heroic effort by the individual, straining against the yoke of what everyone else assumes that they already know. Any growth in mass consciousness comes about through the effort of many such individuals.

But consciousness by itself is sometimes not sufficient to advance, no matter how extreme the effort. Consider how each of us deals with problems in our lives. First we turn all our traditional conscious tools to bear on the problem, confident it will yield as so many problems have before. However, if none of our usual methods work, and if the problem is sufficiently important that we can't just dismiss it with a shrug, then something new occurs: our emotional energy is diverted into the unconscious. There the issue gestates, until eventually some new approach emerges.

Consciousness develops in spurts, both in the individual and in the species. In the species, as long as our current level of understanding seems adequate to the problems at hand, little change occurs. But when new circumstances emerge, consciousness takes a jump. Traditional Darwinian evolution by natural selection seems to be giving way to a similar theory of evolutionary jumps at critical moments in time.

Perhaps the most original portrait of such a watershed in the development of self-consciousness comes not from a psychologist, but a professor of literature and all-around intellectual gadfly—the late Marshall McLuhan. With the publication of *The Gutenberg Galaxy* in 1962, and even more, with *Understanding Media* in 1964,[10] Marshall McLuhan burst upon the world scene like no other academic has before or since. McLuhan became a media star, and suffered the fate of stars: he was dismissed by serious folk. After all, how important could he be if so many people were listening to him? But, despite the hype that surrounded McLuhan, some of his ideas were of startling originality and concern us here.

In brief, McLuhan argued that Gutenberg's invention of moveable type in the 15th century changed consciousness itself. Before the mass availability of books, sound ruled the world; afterward, sight grabbed the scepter of power. McLuhan was the first to realize what a profound difference there is between those two worlds. A world of sound isn't localized—it's all around us. Sounds come from "here" or "there" or anywhere. Each sound has an importance in itself. McLuhan argued that the first words were echoes of nature, words that imitated nature. Each word was alive in itself, each word was magic.

In such a world, we are hardly likely to develop a strong sense of "I" in opposition to a specific "other" in the world. Aural people are more likely to live in a world of "participation mystique" with the environment. Participation mystique is a term originated by anthropologist Lucien Levy-Bruhl, and was much used by Jung. It describes a state of consciousness both felt was characteristic of "primitive (?) human beings," in which we experience thoughts and feelings as outside ourselves in much the same way that the sounds of the physical world are outside. Though the world is alive with meaning, there is no true consciousness because everything blends with everything else.

---

[10]Marshall McLuhan, *The Gutenberg Galaxy* (Toronto: University of Toronto Press, 1962); and *Understanding Media* (New York: Signet Books, 1964).

> The more limited a man's field of consciousness is,
> the more numerous the psychic contents (imagos)
> which meet him as quasi-external apparitions,
> either in the form of spirits, or as magical poten-
> cies projected upon living people (magicians, wit-
> ches, etc.). . . . (where this happens, even trees
> and stones talk). . . .[11]

With mass literacy, sight became the predominant function, reading the most powerful skill. Books are made up of words, words of letters. The mind has to process letters to make words, then words to make sentences, sentences to make ideas. Just as letters can be arranged in many different ways to make words, we come to regard words as interchangeable units that make up communications. Words become demystified. After a while, the mind begins to think in this linear fashion. The mind structures reality into sequential chunks of information, like letters in a word, like words on a page. We start to think of reality in terms of sequences of cause and effect, each effect the cause of still another effect. The world ceases to be alive, it becomes a machine.

Yet, paradoxically enough, that dehumanization is connected with consciousness. We become aware that our own identity is separate from all the "things" outside us. As long as aural men and women are locked in a participation mystique with their total environment, they are one with the thunder and lightning, one with the bison they kill or the sheep they herd. Once the universe becomes composed of separate "things," an "I" can form that isn't any of those things.

The world around us (and in us for that matter) is continuous. There are no boundaries in reality except those created by consciousness. A mountain is only a

---

[11]Carl Jung, *Collected Works*, Vol. 7, 295.

mountain because we have chosen to separate it from its surroundings. An animal is only a separate entity because we have defined it as such. If our vision was much more precise, we could just as readily have defined each skin cell as a separate entity. Or if we "saw" reality with heat detection, we might define parts of an animal as wholes, or perhaps a herd of animals as a whole. Consciousness is a moveable frame, defined in large part by our existence as sensate beings with very particular sensory limitations.

Consciousness cuts the totality of the world into little pieces of a size able to be assimilated by our relatively primitive brains. But whatever appears in consciousness has to begin as an inchoate image in the unconscious that only slowly emerges into consciousness. Picture consciousness (in the broadest sense of the word) as the light in a movie projector. What appears on the screen to be a moving picture is really a projection of a series of individual snapshots. The motion we think we see in a movie is really only the result of our sensory limitations; i.e., if the time interval between frames is short enough, our brains think the two scenes are continuous and interpret any differences between the two scenes as motion. Consciousness is a light (that's the mystery, isn't it?) that projects snapshots of reality, each static in itself. These snapshots pass through our minds so rapidly that they give the illusion of motion and continuity.

Now, of course, consciousness of self didn't actually begin in the 15th century. We have always possessed some degree of self-consciousness. But McLuhan identified a watershed in human history, a point at which *mass consciousness* began, and he connects it with sight. As we have already seen, the most recent of Paul MacLean's three brains, the neocortex, might fairly be termed the visual brain, so heavily is it connected with vision. And this most recent brain still goes back fully three million years!

As humanity came to depend more and more on vision, it was inevitable that some degree of consciousness (in Jung's sense of the word) would probably begin to appear. And it undoubtedly took a quantum leap among those who were literate. However, before moveable type, consciousness was limited to the fortunate few; most men and women lived their lives unconsciously, like any other animal. At the point when moveable type came into existence, consciousness was evidently ready to leap again, with moveable type as a convenient evolutionary tool.

THE TOTALITY OF MEMORY

What Freud termed simply the *unconscious*, Jung called the *personal unconscious* (to distinguish it from the *collective unconscious*). The personal unconscious is significant enough in itself. It seems to have available every experience of our lives, whether or not these experiences ever passed into consciousness. For example, at this moment, I'm typing words on a word processor. I'm conscious of the words on the monitor in front of me. Usually when I'm writing, that is virtually all that I'm conscious of. I don't hear the drone of the fan in my computer (which is quite loud). I don't hear the softer purr of the air conditioner in the background. I'm not aware of the way my body feels in the chair I sit in (until I sit so long that I realize I ache all over). I don't see the books to the right and left of the monitor, or the wall of books behind it. In short, I'm not conscious of most of the sensations with which I'm constantly bombarded.

Yet all of the other sensations—sights, sounds, smells, temperature changes on my skin—are noticed by my body. And, seemingly, virtually all of them are somehow recorded. Psychologist/hypnotherapist Ernest Lawrence Rossi has summarized a wide variety of research that argues persuasively that our memories are "state dependent."[12] That is, we don't remember isolated little bits of information, we remember the entire environment in which an event took place. Because of this fact, it's very difficult to remember an event in a totally different physical environment. However, if we return the body and mind to a state similar to the state they were in when an event first took place, we can usually reexperience that event as if it were taking place right now.

> Roland Fischer, professor of experimental psychology at Ohio State University College of Medicine, cited as an example the millionaire in the Charlie Chaplin movie *City Lights*. Drunk, the millionaire adored the little tramp who had saved his life; sober, he couldn't remember him.[13]

How we manage to record all that information is another question. In the 1940s, neurophysiologist Karl Lashley searched in vain for "engrams"—localized memory sites. Lashley would train rats to learn some new trick, then destroy parts of their brains, under the theory that when he destroyed the part where the memory was stored, the rats would no longer be able to perform the trick. Instead, no matter what part of their brains he destroyed, the rats could still perform the tricks. In fact, he was able to destroy up to 80 percent of the brain without stopping the rats' ability to perform their trick.[14]

His young colleague, Karl Pribram, hit upon a possible answer some years later: he argued that much of our

---

[12]Readers should look at Ernest Lawrence Rossi, *The Psychology of Mind-Body Healing* (New York: W. W. Norton, 1986), pages 36–56 for a summary of much of the past research in this area.

[13]Marilyn Ferguson, *The Brain Revolution* (New York: Taplinger Publishing Company, 1973), p. 72.

[14]David Loye, *The Sphinx and the Rainbow* (New York: Bantam, 1983), p. 186.

memory is recorded across the entire brain, in an analogous manner to the way a hologram records a three-dimensional image across an entire piece of film.[15] Pribram argues that our memories of events are similarly spread over our brain, and that the brain records the total event— i.e., the entire complex of sensations that we experience at any one time.[16]

I don't mean to deny that the brain specializes. There are definitely locations in the cerebral cortex that specialize in seeing, other parts in hearing, etc. But if the seeing parts are destroyed, the memory of how to see still remains; other parts of the brain take over the tasks formerly performed by the specialist. They may not be as good at first, but they get better over time, as a new specialist develops. It's reminiscent of the way you can cut off the tail of a chameleon and it will regenerate a new one.

We are able to do this because we are not recording individual sights and sounds. Instead we are recording the totality of the moment. Seemingly, *all of the brain records everything all the time*. If parts of the brain are better at dealing with visual stimuli, then it's much more efficient later for those parts to handle the visual memories. But it

---

[15]A hologram is a very special form of photograph that records a three-dimensional image. It has the unique characteristic that any part of the hologram records the entire image. Shining a laser through any part of the hologram produces an image in space of the original solid figure.
[16]Karl Pribram, "The Brain," in *Millennium: Glimpses into the 21st Century*, eds. Alberto Villoldo and Ken Dychtwald (Los Angeles: J. P. Tarcher, 1981), pp. 95–103. The major objection to Pribram's holographic brain theory has been the absence of any detailed explanation of how it could occur. In *The Invention of Memory* (New York: Basic Books, 1988), Israel Rosenfield presents Nobel Prize-winning immunologist Gerald Edelman's theory of "neural Darwinism," which provides a totally different physical explanation for the fact that memory isn't localized. But for our purposes in this book, the essential point of both theories is that they present memory as more complex than a simple storehouse with compartments holding different memories.

doesn't mean that those visual parts of the brain don't have the total experience of an event, visual and non-visual, available to them. Nor does it mean that other parts of the brain haven't also recorded the event, including the visual elements of the event. And, of course, terming something an event is just a division of time.

We still don't understand this process very thoroughly, though neurophysiology is a rapidly developing field. It's possible that my comments are a slight overstatement of the situation, but they are certainly closer to the real situation than any of the descriptions of memory we learned in school.

> Several psychologists have tried to measure the difference between intentional recall and recognition. In one experiment subjects were presented with a list of one hundred words five times. When asked to recall the list, they scored about 30 percent. When, on the other hand, the subjects were asked to recognize the one hundred words mixed with one hundred unrelated words they scored 96 percent correct. This still leaves open the possibility that under more suitable experimental conditions they would have recognized even more, perhaps even 100 percent.
>
> . . . It was also seen that visual memory is considerably superior to verbal memory. On tests of ten thousand pictures, subjects recognized 99.6 percent of them correctly. As one researcher commented: "The recognition of pictures is *essentially perfect.*"[17]

---

[17]Peter Russell, *The Brain Book* (New York: Hawthorn Books, 1979), pp. 163–164.

As we will see many times in the pages to follow, the mind seemingly cannot be limited to the brain. It's highly unlikely that the collective unconscious is somehow stored in every individual brain. It's much more likely that the brain is in large part a communication device rather than a storage device.

THE BRAIN SEEN AS A TV SET

In this light, biologist Rupert Sheldrake gives a wonderful analogy between memories in the brain and programs in a television set. Imagine you were watching a TV show for the first time with no idea of what a television was. At the most primitive level, you might think that there were actually little people in the set. As you examined the set, you would quickly discard that overly simple explanation. You would notice that there was a great deal of equipment inside the set. Raised as we are on the wonders of science, you would probably decide that the equipment inside the set created the picture and sound. As you turned the knob and got different pictures and sounds, you would probably become more convinced of your argument. If you took a tube out of the set and the picture died, you would probably feel that you had convincingly demonstrated your case.[18]

Suppose that someone told you what actually happens—that the sounds and pictures were coming from a distant location, carried on invisible waves that could somehow be created at the distant location, be received by your TV set, and transformed into pictures and sounds. You'd probably find such an explanation to be ridiculous. At the very least, it would seem to disobey Occam's razor;

---

[18]Rupert Sheldrake, "Mind, Memory and Archetype," *Psychological Perspectives* (Spring 1987), pp. 19–20.

i.e., it's much simpler to have the pictures and sounds created by the TV set than to imagine invisible waves.

However, you might be willing to come around if you were told several other things about TV sets. First, you might be told that millions of other people had TV sets just like yours and each of their sets could all do all the things yours could. You'd find that fascinating, but it wouldn't shake your argument. After all, each of those sets would undoubtedly be manufactured to produce these wonderful pictures and sounds. However, how could you explain that each of the million sets could get the same program at the same time?

The capper to that might come if the channel of your set was turned to a news program where a reporter told about an event that was happening as he or she spoke. If you then found out that every one of the million sets was able to see and hear about that same event at the same time, you would probably be more open to the concept that your TV wasn't a storage unit, but a receiver of information carried on invisible waves.

Well, the collective unconscious contains information that can be accessed by anyone at any time. It appears to have no limits in time or space. That is, it can access information that was recorded by primitive people, or it can access information about events that have not yet taken place in your life. I'm afraid that the collective unconscious won't fit into an individual brain very well.

THE DYNAMICS OF CONSCIOUSNESS

Let's return to the personal unconscious. Consider reading. At some time in your life, you had to learn the alphabet. You sat in a classroom while the teacher pointed to the individual letters, then said them out loud. You and your classmates repeated the letters over and over, with the monotonous repetition that only the very young can endure. Then you carefully copied each of the letters in your notebook. You copied the letters over and over until you knew exactly what an "A" looked like, and how it differed from a "B" and a "C" and so forth. Then you learned how the letters combined to make words. You slowly sounded out each letter of an unknown word until you could pronounce the whole word. If you already knew the word, your task was done. If you didn't, then you had to find out what the word meant.

As you got better at reading, you could instantly recognize whole words at a glance, so that you didn't have to go through them letter by letter in order to spell out a word. For most of us, that speedy recognition made reading a joy instead of a chore. We became readers. For some, that speedy recognition never came. In any case, for all of us, it took a great deal of time and effort to learn how to read.

Once the ability to read was acquired, you probably spent a great deal of time using that ability. I've never seen any statistics, but I would imagine that highly literate people might spend half their waking hours reading one thing or another. But how much of that reading time is conscious? I'd venture to say very little. For fast readers, the words flow by *without any conscious awareness of their passage*. The words flow straight from the book to the unconscious without any conscious intervention!

I have purposefully picked a controversial example to make my point. You might argue that you are conscious when you are reading, but it's a low level of consciousness most of the time. I would have a difficult time disagreeing with you. But how about driving a car? Like learning to read, it took a good deal of time and effort to learn how to drive. For most of us in the Western world, it's a critical skill. We must drive. If we make mistakes while driving we can kill ourselves and others. Yet how much conscious attention do we pay to driving most of the time?

When I'm driving a route I know well, I turn my consciousness to a myriad of other things, confident that some other part of my mind will take care of the driving. Have you ever driven past the exit you wanted on the freeway, or taken the old route the day you had to go someplace different? How could you do that if you were conscious of driving? If you weren't conscious, who or what was doing the driving?

So, are we conscious when we read or drive, or not? Clearly, the relationship between consciousness and the unconscious forms a complex dynamic that doesn't easily yield an answer.

ARCHETYPE AND COMPLEX

It was this dynamic relationship between conscious and unconscious that Jung observed and described. While working as a young doctor at the Burgholzli Mental Clinic in Switzerland, Jung conducted some word association experiments where he recorded the patient's response to a stimulus word and also measured the reaction time of the response. When he analyzed the results, he found that the responses with the longest reaction times tended to cluster around subjects that had emotional significance for the patient. For example, if the patient had difficulty in dealing with the father, the responses that came the slowest would turn out to have some association for the patient with the father. That doesn't mean that the stimulus words had to be directly connected with the concept of father; they just had to be connected with father in the patient's mind. In our example, most people would associate the word *milk* with the mother rather than the father. However, if the patient had once spilled milk and been reproached by the father, milk might be such a stimulus word.

Jung termed these clusters of emotionally loaded concepts "complexes." As I've mentioned earlier, this concept of a complex appealed to Freud and was one of the early reasons for his interest in Jung. Freud theorized that all complexes revolved around sexually significant events from early life. He reasoned that the process of psychoanalysis should be able to bring the personal associations to mind one at a time. Eventually the chain of associations would lead back to a sexually charged event from childhood. Once the patient uncovered the primal event that lay at the root of the complex, there would be nothing left in the complex and the patient would be cured. This is a logically tidy theory that, unfortunately, doesn't match the facts.

When Jung explored his patients' complexes, he found something quite different. The patient didn't automatically get well when all the personal associations had been brought to light. Nor was there always (or even frequently) a primal event at the core of the complex. Instead, Jung found that after everything personal was made conscious, there still remained a core of incredible emotional power. Instead of defusing the energy, the energy increased. What could form such a core? Why did it have such energy?

It seemed that there must be an impersonal nucleus within a complex. In the discussion of Paul MacLean's concept of the triune brain, we see that our brains contain evolutionary history within their very structure, and that ancient structure still controls much of the life we think that we live so consciously. (See fig. 3 on page 38.) In order to do so, those structures must be highly organized, so that they can be accessed as needed. If our evolutionary past is stored within us (or at least available for us to access as if it were stored within us), there are only two

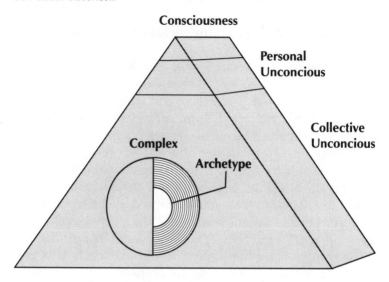

Figure 3. The structure of the psyche. Consciousness, only a tiny part of the psyche, is a recent development. Beneath it lies the personal unconscious and below that lies the vast expanse of the collective unconscious. All sensory experience is first filtered through the building blocks of the collective unconscious—the archetypes—which gather our life experiences around them to form complexes. Peeling away the personal experiences that make up a complex to find the archetype within is like peeling away the layers of an onion.

ways they can appear in our lives: 1) *through behavioral actions in the outer world*—that is, what we normally term *instinct;* and 2) *through images in our inner world*—which Jung initially termed *primordial images* and later *archetypes* (from the Greek for *prime imprinter*).

> . . . there is good reason for supposing that the archetypes are the unconscious images of the instincts themselves, in other words, that they are patterns of instinctual behaviors. . . . The hypothesis of the collective unconscious is, therefore, no more daring than to assume there are instincts. . . .

> The question is simply this: are there or are there not unconscious universal forms of this kind? If they exist, then there is a region of the psyche which one can call the collective unconscious.[19]

As we can see from Jung's comments, he came to use the term *archetype* to mean a formless pattern that underlay both instinctual behaviors and primordial images. For example, at the core of a father complex is a father archetype. For a particular patient, the father archetype gathers about itself images and behaviors of the father that are available from the patient's experience. As one digs deeper into the complex, the images and behaviors found tend to be less personal and more rooted in the experience of the patient's cultural heritage, whether or not the patient has any personal knowledge of the image or behavior.

Unfortunately, a wonderful word like archetype seems far too philosophic and literary for modern scientists; it brings up images of Plato's ideal images and other such taboo subjects. Of course, Jung chose the word *archetype* for just such a reason, realizing that long before science, our greatest thinkers were able to peer beneath the cover of physical reality. I would like to substitute still another term for archetype—*cognitive invariant*—a somewhat ungainly term that might be more welcome and intelligible to modern science. Cognition is the mental process of knowing or perceiving, invariant means constant; hence those constants which in part determine our knowledge of reality.

There is currently a flurry of research, cutting across a wide variety of science, which gathers itself under the general term *cognitive science*. Howard Gardner, in his

---

[19]Carl Jung, *The Collected Works*, Vol. 9, I, *The Archetypes and the Collective Unconscious*, copyright © 1959, 1969 (Princeton: Princeton University Press), 91–92.

book *The Mind's New Science*, describes cognitive science as: ". . . a contemporary, empirically based effort to answer long-standing epistemological questions – particularly those concerned with the nature of knowledge, its components, its sources, its development and its deployment."[20]

Archetypes or cognitive invariants fit into any such study, since if they exist, they are definitely "components" of knowledge, "sources" of knowledge, and heavily involved with the "development" and "deployment" of our knowledge of reality. Accordingly, throughout this book, I will occasionally use cognitive invariant interchangeably with archetype, when discussing archetypes in general. I will usually use archetype when referring to a particular archetype.

My favorite example of an archetype (in this case a mother archetype) concerns the late distinguished ethologist Konrad Lorenz and a baby goose who thought Lorenz was its mother.[21] Lorenz won the Nobel prize, in large part for his discovery of the way instinctual behavior is triggered in animals. He found that animals (including men and women, of course) are born with inner predispositions toward certain highly specific behaviors. A particular instinctual behavior may lie quiescent in the animal for years, until the time arrives when it is needed. When that time arrives, this inborn, collective behavior is triggered by specific outer stimuli. Lorenz termed this process "imprinting." (Remember that archetype derives from the Greek for "prime imprinter.")

Now, in effect, Lorenz was resurrecting the scientifically unfashionable theory of instincts, but he provided a

[20]Howard Gardner, *The Mind's New Science* (New York: Basic Books, 1985), p. 6.

[21]Konrad Lorenz, *King Solomon's Ring* (New York: Signet, division of New American Library, 1972).

new piece to the puzzle: by careful observation of how imprinting occurred, he was able to provide the details of how such instinctual behaviors actually operate. For example, while studying the behavior of geese, Lorenz just happened to be present when a baby goose was hatched. The baby imprinted the mother archetype onto Lorenz; i.e., the baby goose decided that Lorenz was its mother. *King Solomon's Ring* contains a marvelous picture of Lorenz walking along deep in thought, with the baby goose waddling behind as baby geese have always waddled along behind their mothers.

Now Lorenz doesn't look anything like a goose. Nor does he talk like a goose, act like a goose, etc. Therefore, the mother archetype certainly can't be stored inside the goose as a picture of what a mother goose should look like. The archetype has to be flexible enough to adapt to a personal experience of mother as different from a normal mother goose as Konrad Lorenz happens to be. That's what Jung meant by insisting that archetypes were formless.

Jung encountered archetypes from the outside in, through his study of the complexes. However, as we've seen with the baby goose, it is clearly the archetype which comes first. Imagine a human baby instead of our baby goose. It must contain a mother archetype that it imprints onto its own mother. That archetype seemingly contains the entire human history of the interaction of mother and child, and probably the entire animal history as well. A relationship that has been so important for so long gathers energy, energy which shapes the newborn baby's relationship with its physical mother.

Each baby is unique and each mother is unique. Therefore, each baby has to graft its individual relationship with its mother onto the collective archetype of the mother. For example, at birth, a baby already knows how to suckle. As every bottle-fed baby knows, that behavior is certainly able to adapt to a bottle instead of a breast. Every baby knows how to cry and how to smile. (We've all heard the argument that what we term *smiling* is only a reaction to gas. However, more recent research seems to indicate that a baby smiles as an attraction for its parents.) If a baby cries and finds the mother instantly there to see what the problem is, it will grow up with a different adaptation to life than a baby whose mother ignores the crying and keeps to a set schedule of times for sleeping and feeding.

Over the course of the years it takes to develop from infant to adult, each of us acquires a vast number of memories of his or her particular mother. These memories cluster around the archetype of the mother to form a complex of associations to mother. Essentially we have formed a mother within who has both universal characteristics and characteristics specific to our own particular mother.

When we have to deal with situations similar to those we encountered with our mother, we draw on the mother complex. For example, when a baby girl develops into a 3-year-old child, and starts to do something she knows is bad, she might say out loud "bad girl." That is the internalized mother at work. If she falls down and scrapes her knee, she will run off to her mother for comfort. If the mother is not available, she will probably hug herself as if she was being hugged by her mother.

When our baby girl finally grows to be an adult, she will keep drawing on the mother complex in appropriate situations. If her relationship with her mother has been healthy, she will be able to draw comfort and nourishment when needed from her inner mother. If her relationship with her mother has been unhealthy, she is likely to have difficulty trusting anyone because she will see any nurturing situation through the lens of her own sad experiences.

Remember that the mother complex has as its core a collective archetype of mother that has nothing to do with the particular mother. In recent years, psychologists have begun to study children with terrible family backgrounds who somehow managed to become healthy and successful (frequently termed "superkids"). These children turn to other adults for the love and support they don't get from their parents. Sometimes they manage to find an adult or a special teacher who can become a substitute mother or father. More frequently, *they manage to assemble the mother and father they need* out of the characteristics of a number of adults. That's really quite amazing and only explainable if these children already have some inner template of the mother and the father that they can match to their experiences in outer life.

ARCHETYPES OF DEVELOPMENT

There is no way to decide how many archetypes there are. *There are seemingly archetypes for every person, place, object, or situation which has had emotional power for a large number of people over a large period of time.*[22]

If there are such a large number of archetypes, they must have hierarchical levels. That is, the archetype of mother must be contained within the archetype of the feminine. But the archetype of the feminine must also contain the archetype of the wife, sister, and lover, etc. The archetypes of mother, wife, sister, and lover would overlap at the point where each was part of the feminine. But the archetype of mother would also overlap with the archetype of father at the point where each was part of the archetype of parent. In other words, by necessity, the

---

[22]Interested readers should be aware that this is exactly what Rupert Sheldrake argues is necessary for "morphic resonance" to take place. Those interested in his biological approach to these issues are encouraged to read his seminal and controversial book *A New Science of Life: The Hypothesis of Formative Causation* (Los Angeles: J. P. Tarcher, 1981).

archetypes do not have clear boundaries; each archetype merges into other archetypes at their boundaries.

This is exactly the same situation we encounter within our experience of the physical world. Ducks and chickens and ostriches are all birds; birds and mammals are vertebrates, etc. Some classification system is necessary and useful. But the world itself doesn't fall into categories; we humans impose the categories in order to deal with the complexity of the world. Archetypes are equally beyond categorization, yet categories are equally useful for humans.

Jung could have devoted the rest of his life to collecting and categorizing archetypes, like some early botanist of the psyche. But Jung came to his discovery of the archetypes of the collective unconscious because he was trying to heal patients. Consequently, he was most interested in discovering the archetypes that underlay the process of inner healing and growth which he called individuation.

Accordingly, from the multiplicity of archetypes that we encounter—either in our dreams or projected onto the world—Jung singled out three for special attention, since he felt they represented sequentially the stages of the individuation process:

1) the *Shadow*—the archetype that personifies all those *personal* traits which have been ignored or denied, usually represented by a figure of the same sex as the dreamer;

2) the *Anima/Animus*—the archetype that serves as the connection to the *impersonal* collective unconscious, usually represented by a figure of the opposite sex to the dreamer;

3) the *Self*—the archetype of wholeness and transcendence, sometimes represented by the Wise

Old Man or Wise Old Woman (but which takes a wide variety of human, animal and abstract forms).

Elsewhere I've termed these three the "archetypes of development" since each corresponds to a distinct stage of psychological development.[23] Each is encountered one level deeper in the psyche. We'll discuss each of these stages at some length in later chapters. However, first we will explore a topic that fascinates all of us – dreams!

---

[23]Robin Robertson, *C. G. Jung and the Archetypes of the Collective Unconscious* (New York: Peter Lang, 1987).

CHAPTER 3

DREAMS

*Freud . . . derives the unconscious from the conscious.
. . . I would put it the reverse way: I would say the
thing that comes first is obviously the unconscious. . . .
In early childhood we are unconscious; the most important functions of an instinctive nature are unconscious,
and consciousness is rather the product of the unconscious.*

—Carl Jung

Dreams are a bridge between the conscious and the
unconscious. Jung believed that everything that eventually emerges into consciousness originates in the unconscious; i.e., the unformed archetypes achieve form as we
experience them in our outer lives and in our dreams. It is
not sufficient to look at the events of our lives causally, we
also have to look at them from a teleological point-of-view.
That is, not only are we pushed forward by our past
actions, we are also pulled forward by the actions we need
to take, many of which are contained within us as archetypes.

> Because dreams are the most common and most normal expression of the unconscious psyche, they provide the bulk of the material for its investigation.[1]

In his practice as a psychoanalyst, dreams were readily available as the primary raw materials Jung used to explore the unconscious. As we discussed in chapter 1, it was Freud's insistence on the significance of dreams that first attracted Jung to psychoanalysis. Jung's discovery of mythological referents in dreams led to his concept of the collective unconscious and its building blocks—the archetypes. Jung was driven ineluctably to his model by the simple fact of his insistence on honoring the dream and reporting what he found.

The idea that there was a collective underpinning to the psyche that interacts with consciousness, and which we can observe in dreams, isolated Jung from his peers. This was much like Jung's experience with his fellow students in college with respect to psychic phenomena. It is always easier to dismiss strange results than to look at such material in a totally fresh light. In the previous chapter, we have seen that psychological reality is a good deal more complex than supposed common sense would imagine it to be. We have seen that animals (including human animals like you and me) are born with the ability to access behaviors and images that have evolved across the vast history of their species (and all the species that preceded them). And these aren't just piled up haphazardly in some dusty attic of "racial memory," they are organized so carefully that they can be activated at predetermined points in our development.

---

[1]Carl Jung, *The Collected Works,* Vol. 8: *The Structure and Dynamics of the Psyche,* copyright © 1960, 1969 (Princeton: Princeton University Press), 544.

Figure 4. Joseph was able to interpret the Pharaoh's dream, which had baffled the court magicians, because Joseph understood that dreams are symbolic, not literal. (*Joseph Interpreting Pharaoh's Dream*, from *Nuremberg Chronicle* by Schedel, 1493.)

Jung called these inherited behaviors and images archetypes, and I have suggested the alternative term of cognitive invariants. He stressed that these archetypes are formless until they are activated in our lives (i.e., the imprinting process that Konrad Lorenz documented so carefully). Though we don't fully understand how this mechanism operates, it is clearly highly efficient, as it means that a given archetype (say the archetype of the mother) can operate over a wide variety of cultures in a wide variety of times and places. (Since the archetype seems essentially formless, one possibility is that an archetype is stored as some sort of numeric algorithm, but that is no more than speculation at this early point in understanding the nature of the mind.)

. . . It is only our conscious mind that does not know; the unconscious seems already informed, and to have submitted the case to a careful prognostic examination, more or less in the way consciousness would have done if it had known the relevant facts. But, precisely because they were subliminal, they could be perceived by the unconscious and submitted to a sort of examination that anticipates their ultimate result.[2]

As we discussed earlier, Jung pictures consciousness as a tiny area on the tip of the pyramid of the unconscious. Just past the boundary of consciousness lies the personal unconscious, filled with memories of images and behaviors we have acquired during our lifetime. Past the domain of the personal unconscious we pass into the more accessible regions of the collective unconscious, such as tribal, or cultural memories. Past that, we can penetrate further into racial memories, and even memories of earlier species. Is this really possible? Or is this just mystical nonsense, as Jung's critics would have it? To answer those questions, we have to look into the current state of scientific knowledge about dreams.

DO OTHER SPECIES DREAM?

Dream research has indicated that dreaming is hardly confined to humans. Even an animal as primitive as an opossum, which has changed little in sixty-five million years, dreams. With the exception of the spiny anteater, a very primitive mammal, all mammals dream. Birds also dream, though they spend less time each day dreaming than

---

[2]Carl Jung, *The Collected Works*, Vol. 18: *The Symbolic Life*, copyright © 1980 (Princeton: Princeton University Press), 545.

mammals. Even reptiles sometimes exhibit symptoms of dreaming.

Of course, we can't ask a cat or a dog if they dream. But researchers have found that humans have episodes of REM sleep (rapid eye movement) at roughly 90- to 100-minute intervals during a normal night. In total, we spend about 1¹/₂ to 2 hours a night in these REM periods. These cycles are not limited to sleep; we go through the same *ultradian* (more than once a day) cycles throughout the day, but we are less aware of them. When subjects are awakened during REM sleep, they normally report dreams. These subjects may also dream during non-REM sleep, but this dreaming seems more confused and fragmented.

Other mammals experience similar periodic episodes of REM sleep. There seems to be little difference in the total amount of REM sleep, regardless of how developed or how primitive the mammal. It has been found, however, that carnivores do dream more than their prey.

In all species, the newborn dream much more than adults. This means a newborn human baby sleeps two-thirds of the time, and half of that sleep is REM sleep. This is a total of about eight hours of dreaming a day, or four to five times as much as an adult dreams. But do animals really dream, in the same sense that we dream? All evidence seem to indicate that they do.

> Animal lovers have observed their favorite creatures sniffing, whining, yelping, miaowing, wagging or flapping their tails, moving paws, sucking, licking chops, breathing heavily and evincing a gamut of emotions that suggest dreaming.[3]

---

[3]Gay Gaer Luce and Julius Segal, *Sleep* (New York: Lancer Books, 1967), p. 196.

It is hard not to conclude that the animals are dreaming during such periods, especially as all the physiological measurements (Theta waves in an EEG, rapid oxygen metabolism, etc.) are consistent with similar measurements during human dreaming, once we adjust for differences between species.[4]

THE EFFECT OF SLEEP DEPRIVATION

An episode of "Star Trek – the Next Generation" called "Night Terrors," frighteningly dramatized the effects of sleep deprivation. The Starship Enterprise discovered another Federation starship with a lone survivor. All of the other crew members had committed either murder or suicide in particularly horrible ways. As the crew of the Enterprise investigated this tragedy, they themselves began behaving atypically: snapping at each other, drifting off into reveries, hearing or seeing things that weren't there. This was just the way the other Starship crew had behaved in the last days before their tragic end.

Gradually the crew of the Enterprise came to discover that no one was able to dream any more because something had upset their REM cycles. Thankfully, they found a way to restore their REM sleep. Once again, as in all good "Star Trek" adventures, disaster had been averted at the last moment. At the end of the episode, the crew were all lying down to sleep again, knowing this time they could dream.

Scientific study supports this fictional portrayal. In experiments where volunteers tried to stay awake as long

---

[4]Readers should see Ernest Hartmann, "Sleep," in *The New Harvard Guide to Psychiatry*, ed. Armand M. Nicholi, Jr., M.D. (New York: Beknap Press, 1988); and Gay Gaer Luce and Julius Segal, *Sleep* (New York: Lancer Books, 1967), for much of the material on the scientific study of dreams in previous two sections.

as possible, they became disoriented in both time and space, hallucinated, lost motor abilities and eventually evidenced psychotic symptoms, including paranoia. And, at some point, it became impossible to keep subjects from dreaming; they would spontaneously fall into tiny, split-second periods of REM sleep without realizing they were doing so. When the experimental subjects finally get a chance to sleep, they fall immediately into an especially excited dream sleep, and stay there until they wake. Up to a certain point of sleep deprivation, the period of REM sleep roughly corresponds to the amount they missed during their sleepless period.

In attempts to find out what happens when dream deprivation is pushed still further, dream researchers have experimented with animals, often taking the period of sleeplessness far beyond the limits of human endurance. Like humans, animals kept from dreaming long enough, become disoriented, lose motor abilities, and eventually exhibit symptoms which, for their particular species, could be considered psychotic.

WHY DO WE DREAM?

Let's summarize what we have discussed about dreams to this point. With one exception all mammals experience REM sleep, hence dreams. Birds also dream, but less often than mammals, and reptiles sometimes appear to be dreaming, though this isn't common. Deprived of sleep, humans and other animals become disoriented and eventually psychotic.

Remember Paul MacLean's triune brain model, discussed in the previous chapter. MacLean demonstrates that the human brain contains a sub-brain similar to that of the reptiles, a second sub-brain at the level of development of mammals, and a final sub-brain shared only with other primates. Further, the reptile brain appeared at a time when species had become complex enough to need to deal with instinctual group behavior such as territoriality, ritual, and the establishment of social hierarchies. The mammal brain appeared when there was a necessity for an internal mechanism to govern social awareness and relationships. Finally, the primate brain appeared when higher brain functions were needed to deal with an increasingly visual orientation, and the beginnings of language.

From the above discussion, it seems likely that dreams must have been one mechanism for dealing with increasingly more complex social behavior. We could imagine that the early proto-dreams of the reptiles, which appeared sometime between 150 and 250 million years ago, were probably cold-blooded and unemotional. The rich emotional landscape we associate with dreams must have been largely in place as mammals appeared ten to twenty million years ago; those mammalian dreams must have dealt increasingly with complex social and emotional issues. Finally, in primates, especially humans, dreams should have become increasingly visual and have evidenced at least a primitive language—a symbolic language, perhaps?

If this scenario is accurate, we then have to ask, "What purpose do dreams perform in helping people deal with complex social behavior?" In his book, *Consciousness Regained*, Nicholas Humphrey, an experimental psychologist specializing in animal behavior, offers a start at an answer.[5] He begins with a central feature of dreams that is far too often ignored—*our dream experience is every bit as real to us as our daytime experience!* Now it is true that dreams take place in a phantasmagorical landscape where daytime

---

[5]Nicholas Humphrey, *Consciousness Regained* (Oxford: Oxford University Press, 1984).

rules cease to apply—except one: with few exceptions, our dreams evoke the same feelings of happiness, sadness, fear, lust, hunger, thirst, exultation, awe, as similar experiences do in everyday life.

In other words, dreams center on emotional accuracy, not physical accuracy. It is only afterward, in the cold light of day, that we condemn dreams as nonsensical. While they are taking place, they can be all too real, as anyone would acknowledge who has ever awakened in a cold sweat from a nightmare. This feature of dreams accords well with the evolutionary development of dreams we have traced above—that the first true dreamers were mammals, and that the mammalian brain deals with emotional issues.

We learn largely from doing. Since we experience dreams as real, Humphrey points out that we should be able to learn from our dreams in much the same way that we learn from our daytime experience. He argues that dreaming provides an opportunity to try out behavior in advance, so that when necessity calls for new behavior, we will already have perfected that behavior. Since children have a greater need to learn future behaviors than adults, children should, therefore, dream more than adults. And, in fact, in all species, the newborn dream much more than adults; a newborn human baby experiences REM dreaming about eight hours of dreaming a day, four to five times as much as an adult dreams. It is almost as if the babies were dreaming themselves into existence. Humphrey suggests four categories into which we might expect children's dreams to fall:

1) Experiences which [they do] not know of already, and especially those which [they] as particular individuals might otherwise never get to know.

2) Experiences which [they] will not get to know of in reality until [they have] grown older.

3) Experiences which [they] observe other people to be going through and which are characteristic of the community.

4) Experiences which, whether [they have] had occasion to observe them or not, are characteristic of human beings in general.[6]

In his list, Humphrey concentrates on those experiences that a child has not yet had in actuality. However, as a child grows into an adult, there should become a greater need to incorporate actual life experiences into the learning process of dreams. Accordingly, I would suggest adding at least two additional categories to his list:

5) Experiences from our daytime life which went well.

6) Experiences from our daytime life which didn't go so well.

In the former case, our dreams can repeat and even improve upon our actual actions in order to use them again profitably in the future. In the latter case, dreams can try out alternative actions until something finally works successfully. All six of these types of dream experience would allow not only children, but all of us, to perfect and extend the repertoire of instinctual behaviors available to us at birth, as well as the new behaviors we learn over the course of life.

If Humphrey's theory is correct, then dreams should leave actual traces in the structure of our brains, so that

---

[6]Nicholas Humphrey, *Consciousness Regained*, p. 89.

they can be called upon when necessary in our daily life, just as instincts are called upon. In *Dreams and the Growth of Personality*, psychologist Ernest Lawrence Rossi summarizes research evidence supporting a similar view, especially that of Michel Jouvet:

> In 1975, French neurophysiologist Michel Jouvet theorized that dreams (which he terms paradoxical sleep) release genetic programs . . . which serve to reorganize the brain. His extensive research with cats serves to bolster this theory.[7]

Animals less developed than reptiles proceed almost entirely from instinct. Preprogrammed behavior kicks in to fit almost any situation. But fixed behavior patterns don't deal very well with change; the individual animal needs more freedom of behavior. In that light, the increased complexity of the reptiles evolved to provide the individual reptile with a wider range of possible behaviors beyond those it had hard-wired at birth. Primitive dreaming would have then been tied hand-in-hand with a more complex consciousness that allowed individual adaption to the environment.

In this viewpoint, dreams are a central part of a total system of consciousness, rather than some vestigial anomaly. A wide variety of future behaviors could be tried out during dreams. Dreams with unresolved conclusions would be repeated with variations until some resolution occurred. Dreams that led to unsatisfactory conclusions would occur less often than those which successfully dealt with problems. Every variation of those that seemed to work would likely occur over time.

The complex social and emotional lives of mammals would then be seen as a reflection of increased complexity

---

[7]Ernest Lawrence Rossi, *Dreams and the Growth of Personality* (New York: Brunner/Mazel, 1985), pp. 203–206.

both in consciousness and in dreaming. It wouldn't be a case of which caused which, as much as a reciprocal relationship: increased complexity of consciousness and dreaming leading to increased complexity of behavior, which in turn leads to increased complexity of consciousness and dreaming, *ad infinitum*.

Earlier in this chapter, I speculated that, with the appearance of the neocortex, dreams should have improved upon the emotional complexity available to mammalian dreams. Primate dreams should have become increasingly better at modelling outer reality, especially visual reality. They should have begun to reflect upon experience, rather than just experience directly. Finally, like primate consciousness, dreams should have developed a primitive language, probably a symbolic language. With the expanded development of the neocortex in humans, all of these characteristics should have been correspondingly elaborated in human dreaming. And, of course, that is exactly what we do experience in our dreams:

• a striking visual landscape that improves upon that available in daytime life, because a dream can use any image or color necessary to paint the emotional picture the dream wants to construct;

• all levels of reflection: from dreams in which the dreamer is not present, but merely an outside observer; to dreams where the dreamer is deeply engaged in the drama of the dream; even to lucid dreams where dreamers become aware that they are dreaming, while they are dreaming, and may even alter the dream while they continue to dream;

- a symbolic language so developed that it can be interpreted successfully on any number of levels, from the reductionistic Freudian approach, to the expansion of Jungian dream analysis, to the variety of eclectic techniques now used by different schools of dream interpretation. What is so fascinating is that it is almost impossible to find an approach to a dream which doesn't yield psychic gold to the dream explorer.

In other words, the characteristics of human dreams exactly match what we would expect from examining the history of the brain's development. In the light of that history, Jung's contention that our dreams can access information acquired not in our lifetimes, but in the lifetime of our species, becomes much less far-fetched. His model of conscious and unconscious, interacting in dreams, becomes a reasonable description of the reality which closely matches scientific knowledge at this point in time.

Accordingly, I will assume that Jung's respect for dreams needs no further defense and will spend the rest of this chapter unashamedly discussing the practical significance of dreams. My examination will barely skim the surface of dream work, but I hope it will at least encourage readers to pay closer attention to their own dreams.

DREAMS AND CONSCIOUSNESS

Deeds were never invented, they were done. Thoughts, on the other hand, are a relatively late discovery. . . . First [man] was moved to deeds by unconscious factors, and only a long time afterwards did he begin to reflect upon the causes that had moved him; then it took him a very long time indeed to arrive at the preposterous idea that he must have moved himself — his mind being unable to see any other motivating force than his own.[8]

As we have seen, consciousness is a very recent phenomenon. For millions of years, animals, and even humans, have managed to be born, live, and die without the full awareness of self we think of as consciousness. We can feel joy and sadness, hope and fear, without being conscious of ourselves experiencing those emotions. The lack of consciousness doesn't create robots, moving inexorably to a pre-defined plan; the dynamics of the unconscious are much more complex than that.

Although archetypes necessary to our development are already in place when we are born, nevertheless no two humans (or other animals) have ever experienced those inherited behaviors and images in an identical way. Despite the fact that unconscious forces underlie our behavior, our lives are filled with choices (though we remain unconscious of many of those choices). However, it is nonetheless true that consciousness does definitely bring something new to the game of life.

The reason why consciousness exists, and why there is an urge to widen and deepen it, is very simple: without consciousness things go less well. This is obviously the reason why Mother Nature deigned to produce consciousness, that most remarkable of all nature's curiosities.[9]

Whether or not consciousness is nature's crowning achievement, it is certainly its newest novelty. No one respected consciousness, and the individual's heroic attempts to increase that consciousness, more than Jung.

---

[8]Carl Jung, *Collected Works*, Vol. 18, 553.
[9]Carl Jung, *Collected Works*, Vol. 8, 695.

The individuation process, which he carefully studied, each aspect of which we will discuss in this book, is the process of extending consciousness. But all consciousness emerges out of the unconscious, the ultimate mother of all that lives. And dreams stand at that magical boundary between consciousness and the unconscious.

Because of this, major changes in our lives are mirrored in symbolic form in our dreams long before they are evidenced in outer life. This sometimes only becomes clear after the fact, when a long series of dreams can be examined. Frequently, in the period immediately before a major change is going to take place, a single dream will appear which depicts symbolically the entire course of a person's later development. The dream is so rich with meaning that it is impossible to fully understand at the time it first occurs. Later, smaller dreams pick up the individual strands of the changes that are coming. Slowing, ineluctably, they evolve as consciousness grows. Every conscious shift, every conscious resistance can be followed in the cycle of dreams: "We dream a world into being that dreams us into being."[10]

Since there is an ongoing dynamic relationship between consciousness and the unconscious, it is natural that they would react to each other. If our conscious attitude becomes manifestly unhealthy from the viewpoint of the total organism, the unconscious will compensate. To consider a physical example, if the body detects a need for a trace element that has been missing from our diet, we tend to grow hungry for some food containing that missing chemical. Of course, living as so many of us do on hurriedly grabbed fast foods, we are not as aware of our body's messages as we would be if we were still living closer to nature. But all of us have, at some time or another

---

[10]Richard Grossinger, in *Dreams are Wiser than Men*, ed. Richard A. Russo (Berkeley: North Atlantic Books, 1987), p. 191.

in our lives, suddenly developed a craving for food not normally in our diet—a vegetable perhaps, even if we would ordinarily shun that vegetable.

This process appears to go on not only physically but within our psyche. Just as the body is constantly working to promote health and wholeness, so is our psyche. Accordingly, Jung felt that the primary function of dreams was to serve as an unconscious compensation to our conscious attitude. Of course, he means adult dreams, since there is no need for compensation until there is some consciousness to compensate for. Thus, Jung's view complements that of Humphrey presented in the last chapter, rather than contradicting it. In children, dreams are largely the playgrounds where future behavior and attitudes are tried out. As with adults, they are also the school where we learn appropriate modes of behavior and unlearn modes that don't work. As we become adults, there is less need for learning future behavior, more need to develop our full potential.

> In this regard there are three possibilities. If the conscious attitude to the life situation is in large degree one-sided, then the dream takes the opposite side. If the conscious has a position fairly near the "middle," the dream is satisfied with variations. If the conscious attitude is "correct" (adequate), then the dream coincides with and emphasizes this tendency, though without forfeiting its peculiar autonomy.[11]

For example, if people become a little too cocky, a little too sure that they have "the world by the tail," they are likely to dream of getting their comeuppance. If they underrate someone, their dreams might present the despised person as an exalted figure, even a god. Unfortu-

---

[11]Carl Jung, *Collected Works*, Vol. 8, 546.

nately, things are rarely that obvious. Our conscious attitudes are more likely to be a complex mixture—some attitudes right on the money, some wildly out of line. Nor does life stand pat: attitudes which have been fine in the past may be inadequate in the present. Finally, there are few situations in life which don't require us to be able to hold both sides of an issue in mind, in order to judge the situation fairly. Life isn't easy.

THE UNCONSCIOUS NATURE OF DREAMS

> The dream . . . cannot produce a definite thought unless it should cease to be a dream. . . . The dream . . . manifests the *fringe of consciousness*, like the faint glimmer of the stars during a total eclipse of the sun.[12]

Since dreams exist at the boundary between consciousness and the unconscious, once we record and interact with our dreams, a bridge begins to form between those two regions. With more rapid access between conscious and unconscious, growth and change accelerates. Once we become aware of our dreams, they react to our awareness. Then we observe their reaction and react in turn.

Some psychologists have theorized that dreams are not intended to be examined that way, and that doing so may cause damage to the psyche. In my experience, we don't have to worry that we will damage the natural process of growth. The unconscious seems to take care of that automatically. If the dreamer is not ready for some new piece of self-knowledge, he or she can examine the dreams and never notice the critical element. It goes by as if he or she had never seen it at all.

---

[12]Carl Jung, *Collected Works*, Vol. 18, 511.

This is because the unconscious is just that: *not conscious*; i.e., that which we are not yet able to be conscious of. Years ago, a friend attended a weekly dream group, led by a wonderfully elfin Jungian analyst, who I'll call Theodore here. One night he presented a recent dream of his own to the group. My friend had an insight into the dream, and was able to help Theodore understand what the dream was about. The explanation clicked immediately with Theodore. He knew it was important and repeated the explanation over to himself several times.

Later in the evening, he asked my friend if he would tell him again what he had said about the dream. He had forgotten it completely. As soon as he heard the explanation, he said, "of course, of course," and repeated it out loud to himself. Still later in the evening, with some embarrassment, he again asked my friend if he would mind repeating the explanation. Finally, as everyone was starting to leave at the end of the evening, Theodore plaintively asked him if he would mind going over it one final time. Clearly, if something is unconscious, it is very hard to make it conscious.

WORKING WITH YOUR DREAMS

No amount of skepticism and criticism has yet enabled me to regard dreams as negligible occurrences. Often enough they appear senseless, but it is obviously we who lack the sense and ingenuity to read the enigmatic message. . . .[13]

Honor your dreams. It is more important to record them and review them than it is to figure out what they mean. Dreams are so filled with meaning that it is unlikely

---

[13]Carl Jung, *The Collected Works*, Vol. 16: *The Practice of Psychotherapy*, copyright © 1985 (Princeton: Princeton University Press), 325.

you can ever fully exhaust the meaning of even a single dream. That is an inevitable result of their coming from the unconscious. Any dream presents material that you are able to be consciously aware of, material at the edge of consciousness, and also material so far from conscious-ness that you may never become aware why it is present in the dream.

Any person or object in a dream may represent either that actual person or object, or may be used as a symbol of some quality within your own personality. But normally you should assume the latter in working on your dreams, since dreams usually speak in symbolic terms. When you have dealt with enough dreams, you will often get a feel-ing for when they are speaking objectively rather than symbolically.

Pick out people and objects in your dreams and con-sider them as symbols. That is, look at everything you associate with that person or object. Try to determine which associations have the strongest significance for you first, but don't ignore any associations you may have. You are not trying to reduce the dream to a single explanation; rather you are trying to "amplify" it until it starts to reso-nate inside you in a powerful way. Remember that true dreams began with our mammalian ancestors, and are rooted in emotion. Accordingly, trust your emotions in judging when you are on the right track. Don't let your rational mind force you to a conclusion that your feelings disagree with.

It is helpful to have a good dictionary to look up the etymology of the word for an object or action in your dream. This is not in contradiction to what I have said about trusting emotions over thoughts in dealing with dreams: you are not looking for a single unique definition of your dream symbol; you are looking for the historical development of a symbol. Words are true symbols, carry-ing their whole history within themselves. If this sounds strange, just try it for a while and see if it doesn't frequently illuminate a dream that otherwise seemed inexplicable.

> The first time a dream occurs, it may seem superficial and banally repetitive. The second time may be a month later or even forty years later. Existentially it is the same dream. . . . As the process continues, the dream may finally be as brief as to achieve its utterance in a single note, a hiatus between the dreamer and semi-shrouded form, a face linked with a sound and then darkness. It is almost impossible to transcribe such a dream in language; it is a hieroglyph.[14]

Again because of the symbolic language of dreams, they frequently speak in puns. For example, pioneer dream researcher Dr. Henry Reed once did a study of shoe dreams. He found that they most often occurred at critical transitional points in a person's life, when we need to reexamine our "standpoint," our basic view of life. That is, our shoes are the point where we stand on the earth; hence, our "standpoint." If that sounds like a ridiculous pun, try it when you have a shoe dream.

Take another example (just as an example, don't assume that you can plug in a canned definition for a dream symbol): a common dream motif is to find yourself without any clothes. Play with that a little. You're naked, bare, exposed. Ah, that last one might ring a bell. Perhaps you have revealed too much and feel "exposed" in your life. But, of course, everything about the situation adds to the significance. Were you alone and naked in the dream? Surrounded by other people? Were you embarrassed in

---

[14]Grossinger, in *Dreams are Wiser than Men*, p. 205.

the dream? Or did you feel relaxed and comfortable in your exposure?

A patient once dreamed of digging up turnips from the earth of an alien planet. As we discussed the dream, he realized that "turnips" were a pun for "turn-ups," i.e., that which he was turning up from the ground of the unconscious in his dreams. Puns occur so frequently in dreams that it is important to look for them constantly. However, every person has his or her own dream vocabulary, and people vary widely in the type and frequency of puns.

Remember Jung's discovery that dreams often repeat mythological themes. If some element in your dream reminds you of a myth (or fairy tale), read that myth and see if it doesn't help explicate your dream. Sometimes the structure of a dream will be so similar to a particular myth that this will be obvious. In those cases, it is helpful to carefully compare your dream with the myth in order to see how your personal version varies. The myth will give you a feeling for the general problem you're dealing with. Your personal variations will tell you a great deal about your unique angle on the problem.

Famed family therapist Carl Whitaker drew on this function of the unconscious in working with new patients. One of his favorite tools was to sit with a family and tell them "fractured fairy tales." At first, the family members thought they were hearing a traditional story, but somehow things became more and more distorted as Whitaker talked. Whitaker trusted his unconscious to pick the right tale and to restructure it to fit the situation. What came out was always the story of the family he was treating, though so buried in metaphor that it affected the family members unconsciously rather than consciously.

Trust yourself when you feel a dream is significant; if a dream feels important, it usually is. However, the opposite is not so clear. Sometimes a very important dream will seem unimportant because you don't yet want to face the issue dealt with in the dream. In those cases, give yourself a break and don't force yourself to face the issue yet if you don't feel comfortable. However, be aware that you may want to review earlier dreams at some later point. When you do, you may be shocked at just how important seemingly innocuous dreams really were.

For example, when a therapist was first discovering Jungian psychology, he became a "true believer," like many another convert to a "new faith." At that time, he dreamed that he was a salesman for Fundamentalist, psychoanalytic records. It would be hard to think of a better picture of a distorted conscious attitude. But, at the time, he didn't have the slightest idea what that dream was about.

Try unusual ways to connect with the dream. You can close your eyes and try to go back into the dream. If successful, return to some part of the dream that confused you and continue the dream. This is basically the technique Jung originated (at least in the modern Western world), which he called *active imagination*. This seems a singularly apt term because, unfortunately, most of us have been taught to disdain fantasy, daydreams, imagination itself, as idle wastes of time. The idea that imagination and fantasy can be active is quite alien to modern Western thought.

There are many variations on the technique; for example, have a dialogue with the people or objects in your dream. One good way of doing this is to use the "two chair" technique pioneered by Fritz Perls, the founder of Gestalt psychotherapy. Place two chairs facing each other, then sit in one and imagine the person (or object) from your dream in the other chair. Say whatever comes to mind to that person. Then move to the other chair and pretend you are the other person (or object). Respond to yourself. Move back and forth between the two chairs to continue the dialogue. You will find this much easier to do than you might imagine. If you use this technique, try and record it on a tape recorder and later transcribe it into your journal.

Or forget the tape recorder and have the dialogue on paper. Try and relax first. If you know how to meditate, do so for a moment to center yourself. If you don't, here is an easy method. First sit comfortably and close your eyes. Become aware of your feet – pay no attention to the rest of your body. From there, move your awareness to the top of your head. Then to the middle of your chest. Move it around to other parts of your body until you feel comfortable about locating your awareness wherever you like. Then gently feel yourself as a whole. You will find that your breathing slows and deepens as you go through this process, which only takes a few moments.

Then carry on the dialogue with a person (or object) from your dream as with the chair technique. Except in this case record the two sides of the dialogue on paper. I prefer doing this at a word processor. Others might find that too intrusive and prefer pen and paper. You might also draw, paint or sculpt your dream. Contrary to expectation, this is frequently more effective if you have little or no artistic facility. Or try giving your dream a name, as if it were a short story or play. You can elaborate that process and divide the dream into acts, list the protagonists and the action, etc. This is often very useful as dreams lend themselves to such dramatic devices.

In short, there are many, many ways to help work with your dreams. We will have more to say about specific aspects of dreams in later chapters. But the most important thing is to remember the dream and record it. Unless you do this, nothing else is possible.

Dreams form a record of the individuation process. In the next chapter, we will begin a discussion of the starting point for that process: Jung's concept of psychological types.

CHAPTER 4

PSYCHOLOGICAL TYPES

. . . Since the facts show that the attitude-type is a general phenomenon having an apparently random distribution, it cannot be a matter of conscious judgment or conscious intention, but must be due to some unconscious, instinctive cause.

—Carl Jung

In chapter 1, we discussed how Jung realized that Freud's discovery of the Oedipus complex demonstrated that modern men and women still repeated the themes of classical mythology in their own lives and reflected them in their dreams. He wanted to go beyond Freud's initial example in order to extend the boundaries of psychology by "turn[ing] away from the vast confusion of the present to glimpse the higher continuity of history."[1] Instead he found Freud content to rest with his theory of the Oedipus complex, which soon hardened into dogma.

With his wide-ranging scholarly background, Jung was better equipped than Freud to explore this new terri-

---

[1]Carl Jung, *Collected Works*, Vol. 5, 1.

tory, and did so on his own, hoping to demonstrate his case to Freud. However, as you read in chapter 1, when Jung published *Symbols of Transformation*, which showed parallels between a modern woman's fantasies and a wide variety of mythological themes, it was too much for Freud and he broke off relations with Jung.

Jung wasn't the first, or the last, of Freud's disciples to either reject or be rejected by Freud. Freud was a formidable father figure who tended to see his followers as his sons. That attitude eventually forced many of the more independent psychoanalysts to break with Freud in order to find their own path in life. Two years before Jung's break with Freud, Alfred Adler broke away over Freud's insistence on sexuality as the underlying motivation for human behavior. Adler was equally insistent that the primary drive was for power in compensation for feelings of inadequacy (the inferiority complex).

Following his "excommunication" from the small community of psychoanalysts, Jung tried to understand why he and Freud had differed so strongly. How was it that both Freud and Adler could be so insistent on a single motivating force? In contrast, Jung felt that we had multiple instincts that drove us in our lives. Sexuality and the will to power were both inborn drives, but neither was necessarily exclusive. Nor were instincts the whole story. He always felt that there was a call from the spirit that determined the course of our lives, and he didn't feel that the spirit was of necessity weaker than instinctual drives. If it was, we would never have built a cathedral.

INTROVERT AND EXTRAVERT

Jung was to find the link between instinct and spirit in the archetypes of the collective unconscious, each of which extended from the highest to the lowest realm of human experience. However, it was of equal interest that Freud and Adler should be unconsciously attracted to opposite "gods," while Jung himself remained a polytheist. It seemed clear to Jung that human beings were pushed and pulled by multiple forces that could not necessarily be reduced to a single force. This led him to look for historical models of human character that could explain people so different as Freud and Adler (and Jung). Just as the cognitive invariants were eternal structures through which the human mind filtered reality, Jung came to feel that there were a small number of eternal human types.

For instance, Freud saw humanity as eternally torn between the pleasure principle and the reality principle. That is, we all want to satisfy our need for pleasures — especially sexual pleasures — but reality puts limits on our ability to fulfill those needs. Clearly, Freud's view puts an emphasis on the outer world, on the pleasures "out there" and the restrictions "out there" (even if those outer restrictions have been internalized).

In contrast, Adler saw humankind suffering from feelings of inferiority of one kind or another. In order to compensate for that *inferiority complex*, we try to achieve power. By feeling powerful, we are able to blot out our feelings of inferiority. Clearly, Adler's view puts an emphasis on the inner world, on our subjective response to outer events.

Of course, any event can be seen from either of the two viewpoints. We can examine what happened in the outer world, or we can examine what a person felt about those happenings. Jung realized that each of us has a predisposition to one or the other of those two approaches to life. One type of person instinctively draws back when the world approaches him or her, another instinctively reaches out toward the world. He called the movement out toward the world *extraversion* (from the Latin "extra" — outside, and "exterus" — outward), and the pull back into oneself *introversion* (from the Latin "intro" – to the inside). An *extravert* is a person whose primary attitude toward life is extraverted; an *introvert* is one whose attitude is introverted.

Both attitudes are so basic, it is impossible to find any form of life so primitive that it doesn't evidence both behaviors. An amoeba views everything it encounters in the world as either food or enemy. It attacks and swallows food, and flees from an enemy. We can regard the former as a movement out toward the world, the latter as a retreat from the world. Higher animals possess these same instincts. In recent years, Hans Selye's studies of the effects of stress have demonstrated how, under stress, our bodies produce chemicals that prepare us to either fight or flee. Since in most modern stressful situations, we are able to do neither, we have no outlet for that extra boost of energy and are left keyed up and anxious a great deal of the time.

Though we are all able to pick either of the two approaches to the world when a situation demands it, we vastly prefer one or the other. The noisy party that an extravert loves is hell for an introvert. The introvert's love for the familiar is deadly boring for the extravert. When introverts get tired, they have to get away by themselves to recharge. In contrast, extraverts have to find people or things in order to perk themselves up again.

Many modern psychological personality tests use dimensions of extraversion and introversion but they view them statistically. That is, these tests assume that everyone has some degree of both extraversion and introversion, but that most people have a fairly even mix of both qualities. People who are strongly introverted or extraverted are seen as a statistically small percentage of the population.

This approach destroys Jung's concept. Jung didn't think that someone had to be as obnoxiously outgoing as the proverbial used-car salesman to be an extravert, or as withdrawn as a Mr. Milquetoast to be an introvert. Those are the two extremes that show up on the personality tests as extravert and introvert.

As with so many things, Jung saw deeper than just the obvious outer behavioral characteristics. To recapitulate: extraversion is a turning outward toward the world for energy, introversion a turning inward toward the psyche. Most of us fall cleanly into one or another of those two camps, regardless of the extremes of behavior which the psychological tests find.

The reason this distinction is so critical is that introverts share a great number of traits that contrast with the traits of extraverts, just because they are introverts, regardless of their degree of introversion. However, because our behavior is frequently more an evidence of societal restrictions than personal preferences, it is often necessary to turn to a person's dreams to find if he or she is introverted or extraverted. If the dreamer is most frequently in conflict with an introverted person, he or she is an extravert and vice versa. This is because the undeveloped attitude has retreated into the unconscious and taken various personified forms. (We will discuss this in more depth in the following chapter on the Shadow.)

THE FOUR FUNCTIONS

Notice that Jung's concept of introvert and extravert handily explained the opposition between Freud and Adler over the primary human drive. However, it did not yet explain Jung's own difference from both. Because Jung himself was both introverted and a brilliant thinker who was somewhat uncomfortable with his feelings, he initially tended to equate introversion with *thinking*, extraversion with *feeling*. It took Jung nearly ten years to realize that the differences between introverts and extraverts were not the be-all and the end-all of human personality. He gradually came to realize that thinking and feeling were different dimensions of personality that were independent of whether a person was an introvert or an extravert.

Once he was free to think of divisions other than introversion and extraversion, he soon realized that many people approach life neither through thinking nor feeling, but through *sensation* itself. (Jung's linguistic abilities stood him in good stead here, since in Jung's native German, feeling and sensation are not clearly distinguished and hence easily confused.) However, there seemed to remain a fourth quality that was not sharply distinguished from feeling in any of the Western languages, but which seemed to Jung qualitatively different from feeling, which he called *intuition*.

The distinction Jung used was to limit *sensation* to information we receive through the sense organs—sight, hearing, taste, etc. *Intuition* was used when we received information straight from the unconscious, bypassing sensation. Since all perception is inside us anyway, the distinction is not as marked as one might imagine.

So, in addition to the two attitude types of introversion and extraversion, Jung now had four functions which we use in dealing with the world: thinking, feeling, sensation and intuition. Sensation and intuition are both perceptive functions. We use them to acquire data which we then process with thinking and feeling. Thinking identifies and classifies the information we've acquired through sensation or intuition. Feeling assigns a value to it; it tells us what it's worth.

Since both thinking and feeling can be applied with reason and discrimination, he termed them *rational* functions. Jung recognized that we have a predisposition toward equating reason with thinking, and dismissing feeling as non-reasoning, because we confuse it with its physical counterpoint—emotion. But feelings (at least as Jung defined them) are not emotions. Someone with a sharply discriminated feeling function can assign a value to something with as much reason and as sharp distinctions as the best thinker can use in placing something into an appropriate mental category.

Sensation and intuition, on the other hand, are *irrational* functions. They are our windows on the world, and as such they provide the data that thinking and feeling need to operate with. In our overly rational times, labelling something irrational is tantamount to condemning it out of hand. Jung intended no pejorative connotations at all when he termed sensation and intuition irrational functions. Each function had a purpose and each was equally valid when used for its assigned purpose. Each was equally invalid when it tried to substitute inappropriately for another function.

Notice that the four functions readily split into two complementary pairs of functions—thinking vs. feeling, and sensation vs. intuition. Thinking and feeling are mutually exclusive: you can't categorize something and value it at the same time. You have to do one or the other. Neither can you turn to your senses for information at the same time as you turn inward for a hunch about what is going to happen. Since we all tend to continue to do what we do best, we settle on one or another of the four functions as our primary function. The opposite function is forced into the unconscious. Jung termed this function the *inferior function.*

INFERIOR FUNCTION

I'll discuss the four functions at some length, but let's briefly consider the inferior function first. Say that we are a *thinker* (here meaning someone whose primary function is thinking). Since we're good at it, we almost invariably prefer thinking to feeling. We will even substitute thinking for feeling in situations that clearly indicate feeling is in order. Our feeling function, not very good to begin with, gets worse through lack of use.

However, since we need something to think about, we are forced to use either sensation or intuition to provide us with the raw materials our thinking function refines into high-grade ore. We will probably settle on one or the other (sensation or intuition) most of the time, but there is no inherent conflict between either function and our primary thinking function. Though we can't sense and intuit at the same time, either fits comfortably with thinking. Therefore, it is quite possible over the years for us to develop both sensation or intuition to a high level of ability, though still subservient to the master function—thinking.

While the other three functions (in our example, thinking, sensation, and intuition) are used consciously, the inferior function—feeling—becomes unconscious. We stop even being aware that it is possible to feel something. When circumstances absolutely force us to feel, our feelings are contaminated with all sorts of unconscious material—good and bad. At weak moments, the unconscious will flood out of our inferior function and overwhelm us. Our inferior function thus becomes our gateway to the unconscious, and the unconscious is the source of everything that is magical and wonderful in life.

If Freud were right, and our unconscious consisted of nothing more than repressed memories, it wouldn't be magical. But Freud wasn't right: beneath those repressed memories (the personal unconscious), lies a vast dynamically self-organizing cavern of collective memory. It seemingly has no limits in time or space; presumably, it can reach into the future as well as into the past. In the present, it can provide information about events thousands of miles away. The collective unconscious connects us with everyone and everything that exists or ever has existed and perhaps ever will exist. (More on this later in the chapter on the Self.)

Every spiritual feeling, every mystical insight, every creative experience, comes from the collective unconscious. Whether there is a God that lies beyond that experience is a metaphysical question that we each have to answer at some time in our life. But there is no denying the *numinous* quality of our experience of the collective unconscious through the inferior function.

Numinous is a word coined by the theologian Rudolph Otto,[2] from the Latin "numen," meaning creative energy or genius. Otto wanted a word that expressed the feeling of awe and mystery that we all experience at various times in our lives. Regardless of our religious convictions (or lack thereof), we invariably experience the collective unconscious as numinous. It might be numinous *and* frightening, numinous *and* nurturing, numinous *and* abstract, but always numinous. That is a sure sign that we are dealing with a more than human aspect of reality.

In her booklet, *The Inferior Function*,[3] Jung's distinguished colleague, Dr. Marie-Louise von Franz, says that the inferior function brings an enormous emotional charge with it. This is because it has all the energy that has been diverted to the unconscious whenever consciousness was unable to deal with something. Because of this, people get very emotional when you touch their inferior function. This can be negative, but it also offers the hope of unearth-

---

[2]Rudolf Otto, *The Idea of the Holy* (London: Oxford University Press, paperback reprint, 1958).
[3]Marie-Louise von Franz and James Hillman, *Jung's Typology* (Dallas, TX: Spring Publications, 1971).

ing a treasure store of emotional depth that we have previously denied or neglected.

Just as it is sometimes difficult to decide whether a person is an introvert or an extravert, it can be equally hard to determine their primary function. This is especially true if they have a highly developed secondary function. In that case, it's easier to find the inferior function and deduce the primary function. The trick is to find which function is most difficult for the person to use successfully.

For example, if you're undecided whether a person is a thinker or a sensate because he or she is good at both, find out which is more irritating—someone who brings feelings into matters that should be dispassionate, or someone who comes up with grand theories? If the interjection of feelings is more of a bother, he or she is a thinker. If someone with grand theories (a mark of an intuitive), this person is a sensate.

If the person is not sure, ask him or her to imagine that he or she is exhausted. What if someone came up with a staff problem (feelings) or asked him or her to provide an instant overview of a project (intuition). Which would frustrate the most? Sometimes it helps to make it personal: have the person describe someone who is really irritating. Almost invariably that person will be carrying the inferior function. I will have more to say on this in the next chapter, when I discuss the archetypal figure of the Shadow.

If all else fails, dreams will provide the answer over time. The inferior function is usually personified in a highly unflattering light in dreams. For example, in the early stages of a Jungian analysis, an intuitive dreamed of having to get past some half-human creatures with no foreheads at all who were squatting on the grounds, gnawing on food, oblivious to the filth around them. That was a dream version of sensates, as only an intuitive could see them.

THE PATH OF INDIVIDUATION

It's easy to misunderstand Jung's purpose in developing a theory of psychological types. We might regard them as an attempt on Jung's part to fit us each into a tiny little box and deny our individuality. However, Jung's purpose was exactly the opposite. Freud had a single developmental path that all of us were supposed to follow. Those who didn't were neurotic. Unfortunately, since Freud was an extravert, his developmental path was an extraverted path. For example, when Jung looked at the characteristics of people Freud regarded as "narcissistic," Jung found that some were indeed self-absorbed and immature. However, others were merely introverted.

Jung came to realize that we can't even begin to understand anyone's proper developmental path unless we recognize that people of different psychological types grow and develop in different ways. Introverts and extraverts have strikingly different paths to follow. When you add the variety of thinkers and feelers, sensates and intuitives, each with their different starting positions in life, it would be remarkable if they didn't become very different people, not because they developed properly or improperly, but simply because they were different people from birth.

This is especially true because of our inferior function. With work and courage, we can integrate our two secondary functions into our personality. However, it is not possible to totally integrate our inferior function because it connects us to the entire body of the collective unconscious. Therefore, trying to integrate the inferior function is like trying to swallow the ocean; it can't be done.

For example, intuitives will never be able to integrate sensation fully into their personality. They will always feel a certain degree of discomfort in dealing with the "facts" of the world. Individuation for intuitives has to be very, very different than for introverted sensates (imagine computer programmers). Now that doesn't mean that intuitives should avoid dealing with sensation entirely—just the contrary. For intuitives, sensation can be the key that unlocks all the mysteries of life. Sensation can offer pleasures that their more familiar intuition can't begin to provide. But they will never have the subtle ease at dealing with sensation that a sensate will.

However, rather than just talking about "intuitives" and "sensates," we need to talk at more length about the characteristics of the psychological types. Let us begin with a more extensive discussion of extraverts and introverts.

THE EXTRAVERTED TYPE

We've already defined the extraverted type as oriented toward the outer rather than the inner, objective instead of subjective. Extraverts are totally comfortable with the world around them because, to extraverts, that's the only world there is. That's both the strength and the weakness of extraverts. It is extremely difficult for extraverts to even be aware of their inner world. When extraverts are quiet, it isn't because they are conscious that they are thinking at all. Introverts can't imagine not hearing a continual dialogue. Extraverts are unaware of this inner dialogue most of the time because they only listen to information coming from the outer world.

Extraverts can never get enough experience of the outer world to satisfy them. They like an ever-changing reality filled with color, noise, action, novelty. They're comfortable with people and like to be around them. Interestingly, extraverts are much less likely than introverts to be aware of their own bodies. Jung says that the body itself "is not sufficiently outside" for them to be aware of it. They tend to bury themselves in tasks so thoroughly that they frequently ignore the body's needs for rest and nourishment. When they are not only extraverted, but intuitive as well, they can become so oblivious to the body's messages that the body is forced to speak to them through illness.

Extraverts can be so attuned to their environment, so aware of the people they encounter in that environment, that they become like chameleons, changing colors to match each new background. Extraverts are always on, always ready to perform in any social setting. They push everything up another notch, adding more energy, more emotion. Listen to the difference between a fish story told by an introvert and one told by an extravert. The extravert's story adds, embellishes, decorates. If reality occasionally gets left by the wayside, well too bad for reality. Introverts are well aware of this life-of-the party characteristic of extraverts.

However, it's critical to realize that because the conscious attitude is extraverted, there exists a compensatory introverted attitude in the unconscious. The more extraverts throw themselves into frenzied projects and relationships in the outer world, the more a pull toward quiet and reflection forms in the unconscious. Marie-Louise von Franz comments that "extraverts, when they come to their other side, have a much purer relationship to the inside than the introvert." In contrast, she notes that when an introvert is able to connect to their inferior extraversion, they "can spread a glow of life and make life . . . into a symbolic festival, better than any extravert!"[4]

As an example of the latter case, I once knew a brilliant computer programmer (hence obviously an introvert). He never said two words when one would do, and preferred to say none if possible. Yet no one was more fun when there was a celebration like an office Christmas party. He

---

[4]Marie-Louise von Franz and James Hillman, *Jung's Typology*, p. 20.

absolutely loved such events. Every year at the party, he put on a silly red and white Santa cap and handed out the gifts to everyone. One would have thought that he would be embarrassed to tears since, in everyday life, any show of emotion was anathema to him. But symbolic events released his inhibitions and he became so joyful that he freed everyone around him.

THE INTROVERTED TYPE

Introverts are quieter than extraverts. Frequently a quick way to distinguish introverts and extraverts is the sheer volume of words used by extraverts. Introverts much prefer the familiar to the novel—they like things to stay the same. They are normally more comfortable with their own company than the company of others. In situations where they encounter new people, they feel lost and out of place. They prefer to go over things in their minds before they actually experience them in the outer world.

In our own extraverted culture, introverts have largely been viewed pejoratively. It's far different in an introverted culture like Japan, where extraversion is frowned upon. Both the introverted and the extraverted modes of adaption to life are both normal—both work. As I have mentioned, one of the things that originally pushed Jung toward his concepts of introversion and extraversion was Freud's condemnation of narcissistic personalities. Jung realized that the label fit some people who were truly narcissistic, but was also unfairly applied to people merely because their orientation was inward rather than outward.

To extraverts, introverts are always going to appear to be selfish and self-absorbed because they are more interested in the inner world than the outer world. For extraverts, it's almost impossible to imagine how introverts can deny the "facts" of the outer world. Extraverts are not even aware that those facts have been colored by their own unconscious inner processes. Introverts are always aware that all they know about the world is how it appears in their minds.

Jung put the position of introverts succinctly: "The world exists not merely in itself, but also as it appears to me!"[5] Classically, the battle between extraversion and introversion was first tackled explicitly in philosophy. The philosophical version of introversion is called the "idealist position." As expressed in the 18th century by British philosopher Bishop George Berkeley: we experience nothing but the thoughts that pass through our minds. Therefore, that is all we can assert about reality. To insist that there is something "out there" is nonsense. All we know is what we experience "in here."

At roughly the same time, Scottish philosopher David Hume denied that most basic tenet of the extraverted position—causality. We just take it for granted that one action causes another. All of classic Aristotelian logic is based on syllogisms (i.e., if A implies B and B implies C, then A implies C). Newton said that for every action, there is an equal and opposite reaction. Or more simply—every effect has a cause. Hume knocked the ground from under causality by shifting the argument to the mind. Say that we argue that a baseball changes direction when it hits a bat because it hit the bat. Hume would insist that all we can really assert is that the ball hit the bat and that the ball went in the opposite direction. Two events were related in time and space in our perception. But there is no logical necessity to prove that one caused the other.

In this view, the subjective is the real world, not the objective. Well, a still greater philosopher, Immanuel Kant, came along late in the 18th century and gave an

---

[5]Carl Jung, *The Collected Works*, Vol. 6: *Psychological Types*, copyright © 1971 (Princeton: Princeton University Press), 621.

answer that previewed Jung's own view. Kant said that there was an objective outer world, but we can only experience it through the filter provided by our minds. We already have inborn psychic structures into which we fit our perceptions of reality. We cannot perceive reality except through those structures. And, of course, we have already encountered those structures in this book under Jung's term of archetypes and my term of cognitive invariants. Kant felt this was a necessary limitation of humanity, that we could never know "das ding an sich" (the thing in itself).

But really even Kant's view is shortsighted. How is it that the cognitive invariants through which we filter reality are so admirably fitted to reality? It's not like we keep running into things we don't see, or burn ourselves by touching objects that appear cold. No, when we experience the world through the cognitive invariants, we seem to have as accurate a map of reality as the human mind is capable of perceiving. The same cognitive invariants must be experienced very differently in a fish, which has a totally different environment and different sensory abilities from a human. But the cognitive invariants of the inner world and the objects of the outer world must somehow be two aspects of the same thing.

We all experience the outer world through the inner world. Extraverts ignore the intermediate process and act as if they were experiencing the outer world directly. Introverts center on the inner process. Because of this, introverts are prone to solipsism (the belief that no one nor no thing exists except the person thinking that thought).

An introvert friend has insisted to me that since he is the one who perceives the world, and he is the one who reaches decisions about the world, that, therefore, there is no world (for him) unless he's thinking about it. It's hard to argue with that position, but an extravert wouldn't bother, because no extravert takes the inner world that seriously. In Boswell's immortal *Life of Johnson*, he tells how Johnson (an extravert's extravert), when presented with Berkeley's argument, kicked a nearby stone and solemnly proclaimed: "I refute it *thus*."[6] Of course, he didn't refute anyone since it was only in his mind that he felt the sensation of kicking the stone, only in the minds of those around him that they perceived him kicking the stone. The difference between extravert and introvert on these topics is emotional—not logical.

The introvert is only comfortable with the outer world once he has an inner model available. Von Franz says that Jung told her about a child who wouldn't go into a room unless he knew the names of every piece of furniture in the room.[7] An introvert once told me that what made him most uncomfortable in a new situation was that there might be some person or some concept presented that he had never encountered before and didn't know how to deal with. Another introvert explained that he felt much more comfortable once he developed a set of strict rules that he used in social situations. He only adapted those rules under the most pressing needs.

Just as the inferior function of an extravert is introverted and attracts the extravert to the inner world, the inferior function of an introvert is extraverted and pulls the introvert toward the outer world. It is important that the introvert actually experience that outer world, not stand behind a screen of inner experience. Hermann Hesse's *Steppenwolf* is a classic portrait of an introvert pulled out into the sensual world of experience. In that novel, a saxophone player stands as the symbol for the introvert's view of the sensual extravert. Today we might substitute a rock star.

---

[6]Louis Kronenberger, ed., *The Portable Johnson & Boswell* (New York: Viking Press, 1947), p. 125.
[7]Marie-Louise von Franz and James Hillman, *Jung's Typology*, p. 3.

I imagine that, by this point, the reader has a better feeling for the two opposite attitudes toward the world. The reader should be able to say with some confidence whether he or she is an introvert or an extravert, and probably be able to identify the attitudes of many others who are significant.

In the rest of this chapter, we will move on to a detailed discussion of the four functions—thinking, feeling, sensation and intuition. Finally, we'll talk about the eight psychological types we get by combining attitude and function. Obviously, we could go beyond that to the sixteen combinations of attitude, major function and secondary function, but we have to stop somewhere!

THE THINKING FUNCTION

Thinkers seem cold to feelers. They approach life dispassionately, with little regard for either their own emotions or those of others. They like tidiness and order and are exceptionally good at arranging things logically. Because of this, they are relatively immune to emotional problems going on around them. They can keep their orderly world going in the midst of chaos.

If thinking people are also extraverted, life is determined by rational conclusions (rules) based on objective data (facts). Because of this, extraverted thinkers make excellent executives—until they encounter the human element, which they consider secondary to logic. Von Franz notes that "this type is to be found among organizers, people in high office and government positions, in business, in law and among scientists."[8]

Their morality is determined by a strict set of rules and people had better conform to that set of rules. Because of

---

[8]Marie-Louise von Franz and James Hillman, p. 38.

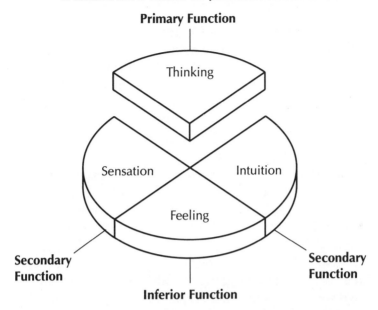

Figure 5. Thinking type. If your primary psychological function is thinking, you will also develop at least one of the secondary functions— sensation or intuition. However, it is impossible to fully develop the inferior function (feeling), which is your gateway to the riches of the collective unconscious.

this we find a lot of reformers among extraverted thinkers. They have a firm code of what's right and wrong, and they're going to implement it come hell or high water. Unfortunately, logical codes tend toward black and white with few shadings of gray, so that there is very little room for human fallibility in their moral codes. More than any other type, extraverted thinkers are prone toward the maxim that the end justifies the means. As an example, there was a surfeit of extraverted thinkers in the original intellectual hierarchy of the Communist Party.

The inferior function of extravert thinkers is not only introverted, but introverted feeling in particular. There- fore, when they do feel something, they are likely to have very tender emotions. Unfortunately, they are unlikely to share those feelings because they are too busy with their careers, but that doesn't make the feelings any less powerful. That's why extraverted thinkers make such faithful friends. Their feelings may be buried, but they are deep and lasting. While they are perfectly willing to move from one new idea to another, they are much more reluctant to change emotional loyalties.

If thinkers are introverted, they are oriented not so much toward facts, as toward ideas. If the facts don't fit the theory, too bad for the facts. That's a powerful position, and it's why so many of those who have changed the world with their ideas have been introverted thinkers. But it is also a dangerously solipsistic position in that there is little reality checking going on. Since introverted thinkers are drawing on some archetypal idea, it is necessarily true at the broadest level, but not always true at the human level. It is very difficult for introverted thinkers to even understand what "true at the human level" means.

Jung contrasted Darwin and Kant as extraverted and introverted thinkers, respectively. Darwin gathered facts about physical reality for decades before he published *The Origin of the Species*. He argued his case by example after example. In contrast, Kant took all knowledge as his province in his "Critique of Pure Reason."

The epitome of introverted thinkers is the proverbial absent-minded professor. Introverted thinkers can be so impractical and so unable to adapt to the world that they are easily exploited. This is especially true if they are male and in a male-female relationship with a worldly woman. Some introverted thinkers say that they have always felt like strangers in the world. Males sometimes have dreams where feminine figures devour them. Frequently, successful introverted thinkers have people who take care of all the worldly things for them.

Their inferior feeling isn't capable of shadings of judgment. Things are yes or no, hot or cold, good or bad. Because their feelings are buried in the unconscious, they move very slowly, almost glacially. But watch out when they erupt! The reaction of others around them is likely to be: "Where did that come from?"

THE FEELING FUNCTION

Just as introverted values have been criticized by our extraverted culture, feeling and intuition have been viewed as inferior to thinking and sensation. Western culture has been overwhelmingly masculine, and thinking

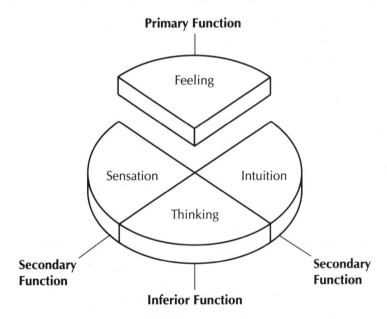

Figure 6.   Feeling type. If your primary psychological function is feeling, you will also develop at least one of the secondary functions— sensation or intuition. However, it is impossible to fully develop the inferior function (thinking), which is your gateway to the riches of the collective unconscious.

and sensation have been the predominant masculine functions. This isn't to say that there aren't women who think and sense very well indeed, or that there are not men who have access to their feelings and intuitions. But in most cultures (and certainly in Western culture), men and women have traditionally accepted specialized roles that have encouraged women to develop differentiated feeling and intuition and men thinking and sensation.

A half-Cherokee, half-Irish medicine chief who I once met said that the first law of the universe was that "everything is born of woman." Women carry, bear, and raise the children who are the future. Men have traditionally been mere appendages to this primary process of human evolution. Throughout history, most women have concentrated their energies on this primary role and have developed the psychological functions they need to properly fulfill it.

Obviously, they would first need to select a proper mate. In part, women have used the traditional evolutionary techniques all animals use: 1) making themselves attractive so that more males will desire them;[9] and 2) forcing men to compete for them in order to select the dominant males for mates. However, to a greater extent than any other animal, men and women have also learned to love each other. In contrast with most other animals, human children are largely helpless for many years. They need someone to feed, clothe, teach, protect them, etc. Women have taken on most of those responsibilities for their children, though they have needed men to help.

Like our close relatives among the monkeys and apes, early humanity solved this problem by gathering into tribes that offered food, shelter, and protection for all, especially for the children. Tribal structures gradually

---

[9]In the animal kingdom, it is often the males who try to make themselves attractive to the females, proof that gender-related qualities are not necessarily fixed.

developed into family structures. In ancient cultures (as evidenced by contemporary tribal cultures), families were frequently polygamous: multiple wives for the dominant males improved the gene pool. These early families were still almost like small tribes, with several generations of a family living together. Over time, the family unit grew smaller until it was most frequently composed only of a husband, wife, and their children. In our own day, the concept of a family has become incredibly varied, as if it were trying to redefine itself. Divorce has led on the one hand to the single-parent family; on the other, to something closer to the tribe, with children having multiple sets of parents related in complex ways. However, in virtually all of these variations on a theme, the mother still functions as the center of the family.

Because of their primary role as mothers, women needed to develop a highly sophisticated feeling function. For example, it's clear that a family functions best as a harmonious single unit, rather than just a collection of individuals. In order to keep that harmony, the mother has to be able to evaluate when the unit is functioning harmoniously and when it is not. Then she has to be able to interact with each family member individually, in a way best guaranteed to preserve that harmony. Both the evaluation and the interaction require subtlety of feeling—the thinking function isn't capable of dealing with such complexity satisfactorily.

Though the above argument is undoubtedly true in large part, it's hardly the whole story. Love, whether between mother and child, or husband and wife, cannot be reduced to such a clinical picture. And anyone who has ever observed animals over a long period of time knows that humans don't have a monopoly on love. Still, love among humans is undoubtedly more complex than love in any other species.

Perhaps the longest term study of adult development was the Grant Study, which in 1937 selected a number of men who "had achieved good academic standing in a highly competitive liberal arts college" (actually Harvard). Extensive biographies were compiled and psychological tests were administered at the beginning of the study and throughout the thirty-five years that the study continued! Obviously, such a long-term study was likely to discover many things which can't be discovered in short-term research. George E. Vallant summarized the study's conclusions in his book *Adaption to Life*.[10] Happily, Vallant has the ability to put complex psychological issues into simple human terms.

For example, Vallant says: "I believe that the capacity to love is a skill that exists along a continuum. . . . [T]he ability to love is more like musical ability or intelligence." He concludes that "there was probably no single longitudinal variable that predicted mental health as clearly as a man's capacity to remain happily married over time," and, "it is not that divorce is unhealthy or bad; it is only that loving people for long periods is good."[11]

So let's not too readily dismiss feeling as inferior to thinking, especially not the highly differentiated evaluatory function that Jung meant by the term *feeling*.

In "The Feeling Function," James Hillman summarizes Jung's position when he says that "the feeling function is that psychological process in us that evaluates."[12] We can acquire information about the world either through our senses or through intuition. Thinking can tell us what that information means, but it can't tell us what it's worth, what its significance is. It takes feeling to do that. It's no

---

[10]George E. Vallant, *Adaptation to Life: How the Best and the Brightest Came of Age* (Boston: Little, Brown & Company, 1977).
[11]George E. Vallant, *Adaptation*, pp. 306–307, 320, 359.
[12]Marie-Louise von Franz and James Hillman, *Jung's Typology*, p. 90.

coincidence that our culture, which overvalues thinking and sensation, should be drowning in information, but lack the ability to sort out what is important within that information. Our government gets bigger and bigger, yet is unable to sort out priorities on any basis other than a balance sheet. New challenges are met with old answers because we can't evaluate what problems and what answers are significant. Feeling is every bit as rational a process as thinking, and we need it desperately at this point in time.

Feelers deal in memories; they understand the present by comparison with past memories. Agatha Christie's great detective, Miss Marple, is the perfect example: she solves the most grisly murders by noticing similarities between the present situation and small events in the life of the village where she lives. Most of the men she deals with find her comparisons ludicrous, yet it is always Miss Marple who sees through to the emotional truth hidden in the confusion surrounding the murders.

Thinkers could never do this, because thinkers deal with more clearly defined categories. Feelers are able to deal with the fuzziness of life. This is why thinking isn't adequate to determine the value of something. There are always infinite gradations of value, and only feeling can adapt smoothly to that lack of definition.

Extraverted feelers are "people persons." They're totally at ease in social situations. They not only fit in well with nearly everyone, their mere presence makes everyone feel comfortable. Sometimes they can be too accommodating, too willing to say what you want to hear, rather than what they actually believe. In fact, they may actually believe what they are telling you is true—at least during the time they're telling it.

To illustrate this point, a patient used to complain that he could never hold his boss to any decision for long. He might go into his boss' office and get an agreement on something. Ten minutes later, someone else could go in and get the boss to agree to just the opposite. His favorite way of dealing with any request for a decision was to "pocket veto" it; his hope was always that things would just work out by themselves if left alone.

When they go to the opposite extreme, extraverted feelers can be the most flamboyant of all people. They are typically only fully alive when surrounded by others. They continually suggest things to do, places to go. When they attempt to think, feelers fall into their inferior function with its connection to the unconscious. Rather than force themselves to do any hard thinking, they are more likely to take on a system of thought whole hog. Their own thinking tends to be primitive: they will use one or two thoughts over and over again.

Introverted feelers are less common in our culture and harder to understand. Since their feeling is introverted, they have no way to express it, except to trusted friends and family, and often not even to them. Jung said that he usually found introverted feeling only among women; I have also known a number of homosexual men with introverted feeling. Introverted feelers keep their strong feelings to themselves. They are the most inarticulate of all people because they have no developed thinking function, and because their experience of their feelings is so personal that they can't express that experience to others. Jung said that the phrase "still water runs deep" must have been invented to describe such people.

Although the face they present to the world may be "childish or banal," and sometimes whiny, the feelings that run beneath the surface may be of profound depth. Introverted feelers are probably the consciences of the world. In this light, von Franz says that they "very often form the ethical backbone of a group."[13] Even though they

---

[13]Marie-Louise von Franz and James Hillman, *Jung's Typology*, p. 48.

are silent, others watch their reactions and pay attention to their judgments, whether or not they express them out loud.

THE SENSATION FUNCTION

We use our senses to pull in the "data" of the physical world, at least the data which are accessible for humans with our unique combination of sensory abilities. Once acquired, we process the data with either our thinking or feeling function. As soon as we have processed the data, our brain extrapolates what it expects to happen from the

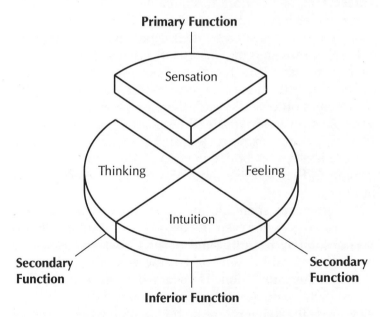

Figure 7. Sensation type. If your primary psychological function is sensation, you will also develop at least one of the secondary functions—thinking or feeling. However, it is impossible to fully develop the inferior function (intuition), which is your gateway to the riches of the collective unconscious.

data it has already acquired. It formulates a plan of action and sends that plan back to the body, together with a "picture" of what it has extrapolated.

The body then acts on that plan, unless the information coming from the senses contradicts the picture extrapolated by the brain. Most of the time, our senses are merely confirming a projection of the brain. We can think of sensation as an active reaching out by the brain rather than a passive reception of physical information. The senses themselves expect to continue the way they have been going, but have to be adaptable enough to adjust when new information comes in.

The extraverted sensation types perfectly mirror these characteristics. They are the ultimate realists, who accept the world as it is, and adjust to it calmly when their expectations are not matched by their experience. As Jung said: "No other human type can equal the extraverted sensation type in realism."[14] In his *Know Your Type* Ralph Metzner suggests that there are two ways nature can make such an adaption to outer reality and, therefore, two different varieties of extraverted sensate: the sensible and the sensual.[15] However, when extravert sensates are functioning at their highest levels, they bridge the gap between those two possibilities. The sensible and the sensual meet in the aesthetic.

I remember spending an afternoon with a charming scientist who epitomized the extravert sensate. His home was absolutely beautiful and he had built every bit of it himself. He and his son had cut the wood, dug the well, and laid the foundation. He seemed to have thought of every detail. For example, since there was a wonderful view from the living room, he built a little wooden holder for binoculars, located where he merely had to reach out

---

[14]Carl Jung, *Collected Works*, Vol. 6, 606.
[15]Ralph Metzner, *Know Your Type* (New York: Anchor, 1979), p. 66.

and there they were. Not only was every normal function of a house accounted for, the house was filled with unique practical devices that he had designed. For example, there was no room for pictures in the library because he had floor-to-ceiling bookshelves. And he liked art. So he put several pictures on tracks connected to the bookshelves. If he had to get to a book located behind a picture, he just slid the picture to a new location.

As the ultimate realists, extravert sensates tend to regard any sort of intuition as nonsense. Von Franz says that they may even go so far as to dislike thought, for even thought interferes with the pure perception of the physical facts of reality. Most are willing to think out loud with others to a point, but then they get tired of it and bring discussion back to physical data, of which they never tire.

Because their inferior function (introverted intuition) connects them to the unconscious, they are prone to fall for whatever the current faddish religious, philosophical, or mystical system might be, whether it's theosophy, Scientology or EST. A large number of extravert sensates are attracted to Jungian psychology for just that reason. They learn a smattering of Jungian concepts and then latch onto the mystical possibilities of the archetypes. Since the cognitive invariants actually are doorways into mystical insight, sometimes this is the perfect choice for them. More commonly, they get swallowed up by the collective unconscious and never manage to apply their inner experience to their outer lives.

Jung's wife, Emma, was an introvert sensate. She once described an introvert sensate as being "like a highly sensitized photographic plate." This type records everything physical in the mind—color, shape, texture, all the detail no one else ever notices. Because all energy is turned to absorbing the surrounding environment, this type can seem as inanimate as a chair or a table to an observer.

When I worked as a therapist-in-training at a halfway home for deeply disturbed patients, I had a good friend who was an introvert sensate. I'll never forget one day when a number of us were sitting in our counsellors' office and a patient burst in. He was screaming in a delusional fashion. He grabbed a chair and smashed it against the wall. All of us were frightened as we knew what could happen when a patient lost control.

My friend merely sat quietly, not even looking at the patient. As the patient continued to yell and brandish the chair, my friend looked gently at him. The patient gradually seemed to become disoriented; he held the chair as if he didn't know why he had it in his hands. His ravings slowed and came in ever quieter snatches. My friend just sat quietly, seeming to absorb all the energy in the room. A few minutes later, the patient dropped the chair and stood utterly exhausted. I was then able to approach him, put my arms around him and lead him from the room. My friend never moved through the whole episode. That's an introvert sensate at his or her best!

I've known a great number of introvert sensates among computer programmers whom I've worked with over the years. They like things to be precise: every detail is as important as every other detail. You don't ask introvert sensates for the "big picture," they haven't got the slightest idea how to get up above the details of their work and see the larger purpose. That bigger picture touches on their inferior intuition and tends to make them very uncomfortable. Yet it is through that intuition that they can find their way to creativity.

Let me tell another story about a computer programmer, who I'll call Ted. One day his department manager found that another programmer had a "bug" in his program that had caused the program to fail and produce a computer "dump" (a print-out of the state of the computer when a program fails). The programmer had spent two days poring over the dump, trying unsuccessfully to find the problem. The manager took the programmer to Ted to see if he could help. He explained the problem to Ted, who just grunted to show he understood. He quickly flipped through the computer "dump," stopped on one page, ran his finger over the page, then stabbed the page with his finger and said, "there." Sure enough he had found the problem!

Yet the same programmer was so isolated from everything except the detail he loved that he became delusional. When he was frustrated, he would get into arguments with an imaginary woman. Then he would stalk off, frustrated at her silliness. I'm sure she was a representation of his inferior intuition trying to talk to him. Unfortunately, he couldn't stand to hear "her." Although few people are cut off from the inner world so dramatically that it personifies as an imaginary person, none of us is comfortable with our inferior function.

THE INTUITIVE FUNCTION

When people encounter Jung's psychological types for the first time, it is usually intuition that stumps them. They understand what thinking and feeling and sensation are, but intuition seems a strange choice to place with the other three.

Intuitives have very little interest in the thing itself, whether it's an object, a person, an image in a dream, etc. What interests them are the future possibilities. They have a nose for the future and can usually sniff out new trends before they become apparent to most people. Where most people see differences, intuitives see similarities. Intuitives see relationships between two sets of seemingly disparate facts that no one else would ever find.

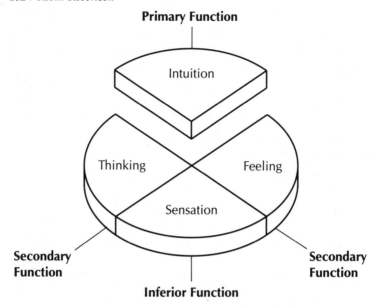

Figure 8. Intuitive type. If your primary psychological function is intuition, you will also develop at least one of the secondary functions—thinking or feeling. However, it is impossible to fully develop the inferior function (sensation), which is your gateway to the riches of the collective unconscious.

Intuitives have no interest in the past; e.g., why something happened. For that matter, they don't even have much interest in the present—in what is happening now. They care only about what is going to happen. Their great joy is in conceiving some new possibility. Once they have the conception, they have little or no interest in actually seeing it implemented in the outer world.

When intuitives are extraverted, they can be the trendiest of all people. They ride the wave of intellectual fashions, always at the crest. If they are able to develop a secondary function of feeling or thinking, they can then slow down enough to make use of that information about the future that they always have at their disposal. If they don't develop a secondary function, they become like butterflies, flitting from one new thing to another, never reaping any benefit from any of it.

Introverted intuitives see the future possibilities not in the outside world, but in the inside world. They are the archetypal models of the Old Testament prophets, of the mystics of all ages and cultures. Certain types of artists and poets are introverted intuitives—artists who are more interested in the vision they have within than in the details of how they capture it without. The great 18th-century poet and artist, William Blake, is the perfect example of a well-balanced introverted intuitive.

All intuitives are likely to be tripped up by their inferior sensation. They deal very poorly with the material necessities of the world—money, sex, food, etc. Extraverted intuitives are likely to spend money as if it were going out of style because it means nothing to them. Introverted intuitives are just as likely to forget there is even any need to acquire money. Usually intuitives are more interested in sexual possibilities than in the act itself, which is likely to be boring to them.

PSYCHOLOGICAL TYPES AS DEVELOPMENTAL PATHS

Jung's concept of psychological types is the starting point for all the rest of Jung's ideas. This book is about the collective unconscious, but Jung's great understanding was that the collective unconscious dwells in each of us. Much of our life is structured by the archetypal symbols that are the organizational units of the collective unconscious. However, the archetypes only become manifest in our lives through the individuation process. And the path of individuation is determined in large part by the type of person we are.

This is not to say that all introverted thinkers, or all extraverted sensates, individuate in the same way. Actually there are as many developmental paths as there are people. But all introverted feelers, for example, grow and develop within certain limits that are unique to them as a class. They all have to eventually find some way to come to terms with their inferior function—thinking—since that is their pathway to the collective unconscious. This is, of course, true not only of introverted feelers, but of everyone. We each have to find our path in life. It helps if part of that developmental path is shared by others like us. This provides at least a partial map of the territory we plan to visit during our lifetime. It is especially important in allowing us to be easy on ourselves in accepting that we don't have to conform to the path someone else thinks we should take.

We will move on in subsequent chapters to the path of individuation itself, using Jung's model of the archetypes of development—the Shadow, the Anima/Animus, and the Self. We'll begin with the Shadow.

CHAPTER 5

THE SHADOW

. . . the aims of the second half of life are different from those of the first.

— *Carl Jung*

Essentially Jung's psychology of the individuation process addresses the second half of life. In Jung's view, we spend the first half of our lives developing a healthy ego, so that we are able to function satisfactorily in the outer world. With that accomplished (and only if that has been accomplished successfully), the second half involves turning away from the world to find our deeper selves. Individuation requires us to pass through both stages successfully. Until we have dealt successfully with the world, we can't hope to find a deeper spiritual side to the personality. (Haven't we all met someone who was sickeningly *good* because he or she was afraid to deal with wanting to be bad?)

Jung developed his model of the psyche through exploration of both himself and his patients. As a working therapist, much of his work involved unresolved issues from the first half of life, usually unresolved parent/child issues. Remember the point we made with the example of Konrad Lorenz and the baby goose: underneath our particular relationship with our mothers and fathers, lie archetypal relationships between mothers and fathers and their children. So a great deal of the actual course of Jungian therapy deals with such issues from the first half of life. Despite this, Jung's psychology overwhelmingly deals with the second half of life—the deeper side of the individuation process.[1]

Dealing with the Shadow, the Anima/Animus, and the Self are all issues of the second half of life. As long as we live largely unconscious lives, there is no opposition between conscious and unconscious. Gradually we evolve our unique conscious personality from the unconscious through our encounters with the world around us—especially encounters with parents, siblings, and loved ones.

Who we are is determined in large part by who we are not. If we are introverted, we aren't extraverted. If we approach the world through thinking, we don't approach it through feeling. However, as we have seen in the discussion of psychological types, we have the potential for broadening our personalities to include other ways of approaching the world. Though we may begin life as

---

[1]Like Freudians, Jungians speak of therapy as *analysis*. In the case of a Jungian analysis, this is a singularly bad term. Literally, analysis breaks something down into its components in order to deal with each separately. Jungian therapy actually involves alternately breaking issues down into smaller issues to clarify them, then synthesizing them into new wholes. And Jungian therapy involves not only rational understanding, but also emotional experience. I could go on and on, but analysis is not a very accurate term. Similarly, by way of comparison with Freud's *psychoanalysis*, Jung called his psychology *analytic psychology*. Again, not a very fitting term, but one which is now unlikely to change.

extraverted feelers, who are interested only in emotional relationships with other people and things, we can certainly develop both sensation and intuition in order to provide food for our feeling function. In fact, if we work hard enough at it, we can develop such discriminated sensation and intuition that it would be hard for a sensate or an intuitive to improve on our performance in those areas. We may even learn to become more comfortable in introverted situations, so that we don't have to turn exclusively to the outer world.

However, in the case of the inferior function (feeling for a thinker, sensation for an intuitive), we will never be able to fully develop those traits, since they are our connection to the collective unconscious, and the unconscious is too big for any human to swallow. But that is an opportunity, not a liability. Whenever we make an effort to improve the inferior function, we are rewarded with a look at the numinous.

PSYCHOLOGICAL TYPES AND INDIVIDUATION

Let's assume that the psychological types we've discussed are either inborn and "imprint" themselves on our lives when we are very young, or at least develop very early even if they're not inborn. That is, very early in life we split into introverts and extraverts, thinkers and feelers, sensates and intuitives.

So there we are at an early age (if not at birth) with a large portion of our personality already in place, ready to express itself in the life we're about to live. As I explained in discussing the inferior function, we like to do things we're good at, and try to avoid doing things we aren't so good at. We consciously develop certain skills, while undeveloped talents retreat into the unconscious.

Of course, things don't always go swimmingly in life. Consider a little girl born with inherent mechanical ability, or a little boy with a natural empathy for the feelings of others (a sensate and a feeler, respectively). One set of parents might have considered mechanical ability in a little girl "unfeminine" and discouraged it. The other might have been equally unhappy with a little boy who was tender and caring, rather than tough and aggressive. When we are children, our parents are gods to us, what they say goes. And if they say that we should be something other than the person we were intended by nature to be, we probably try to change ourselves until we correspond more closely to what our parents would like us to be.

I remember a patient whose mother probably shouldn't have been a mother; she was too childish and selfish to care about anyone except herself. Her little boy was sensitive and loving. His mother alternated between telling him how much she loved her sweet little boy, and then telling him what a horrid little thing he was. And neither response had anything to do with the little boy's actions; it just depended on his mother's mood. In addition, periodically she'd grow bored with being a mother and dump him wherever she could—with his grandmother, an aunt, a friend of the family. When he got a little older, she would actually just take off and he'd find himself alone in the house or apartment. It was then up to him to find someone to take care of him.

Well, that loving, sensitive little boy soon grew hard and suspicious. He grew to distrust anyone displaying affection. As armor against responding to such potentially lethal emotion, he pretended to an ultra-cool disdain for anyone and everything around him. His essential personality had to go undercover. Yet, astonishingly enough, from the first time I met him, I could sense that underlying personality and found that he could bring back his natural trust and love despite all the years of mistreatment. We're a hardy species.

ARE WE BLANK SLATES AT BIRTH?

Let's think about all this for a minute. If we were "blank slates" at birth, and all our knowledge and abilities developed through personal experience, we wouldn't have any undeveloped talents in the unconscious. I wouldn't have found any underlying personality in any patient to bring back from the unconscious. But I did and we do.

Jung used the word Self (capitalized to distinguish it from our normal use of the word) to describe this inborn personality that it takes us a lifetime to grow into. We'll have a lot to say about the Self in later chapters, but for now let's be satisfied with saying that each of us seems to contain a template for the person we are intended to become. This has to be a remarkably flexible template, since it has to fit us at every stage of our life from birth until death. It has to be flexible enough to adapt to the many ways each of us can achieve our destiny.

Yet it can also be remarkably specific. The University of Minnesota has done a study of identical twins which provides a great deal of information about just how far we are from being "blank slates" at birth. Peter Watson summarized the results of this study in his book *Twins: An Uncanny Relationship?*[2] In the December 26, 1982 issue of the *Los Angeles Times*, Watson told a story from his book, about identical twin boys, born in 1939, who were adopted by different parents (the Lewises and the Springers); neither twin knew of the existence of the other.

The coincidences in their lives were remarkable. Both had the same interests and dislikes at school, had worked

---

[2]Peter Watson, *Twins: An Uncanny Relationship?* (New York: Viking Press, 1982).

at the same jobs, had the same habits, the same illnesses, the same hobbies. These similarities were so exact that it would be very difficult to explain them just by the knowledge that identical twins have the same genes. In fact, some of these similarities were so marked, they seemed beyond any explanation of genetic makeup. For example:

> Both had married a woman named Linda, divorced her, then married a second time, to a woman named Betty. Lewis had named his first son James Alan. Springer had called his son James Allan. Both had owned a dog as a boy, and named it Toy.[3]

How in the world could we be born with a plan specific enough to tell us to marry women named Linda and Betty, to name a son James Alan, and to name a pet dog Toy? It's a mystery, but this example points out just how difficult it is to deny our inherent destiny, the path toward the Self we are intended to become.

Jung liked to compare an archetype to a riverbed which has been slowly formed over thousands of years. Originally, there was just a stream of water that followed the path of least resistance on its way to the sea. The water followed any of a number of different branches, one as likely as the next. However, as time slowly passed, it became less and less likely that the water would take any path other than the one already traced many times previously.

However, if circumstances changed drastically enough, a new path could still form. For example, if a rockfall dammed up a portion of the river, the water would be forced to take a new direction. If it eventually branched back into the old path, at least it would have taken a new route for part of the journey. But perhaps part

---

[3]Peter Watson, *Twins,* p. 22.

of the river never made it back to the old bed and a new tributary formed.

So, too, with the cognitive invariants of the collective unconscious, and, specifically, with the archetype of the Self that determines each of our individual destinies. Many of us spend a lifetime struggling against our destiny, stuck in a stagnant swamp, far away from the river that could lead us to the ocean. And if we want to escape that quagmire, we have to be willing to face our first challenge – the Shadow.

WHY THE SHADOW APPEARS

Let's return to the example of the little girl with mechanical ability, and the little boy with a developed feeling function. If the parental pressures are strong enough, the girl will probably forget about tinker toys and erector sets, and turn her interests to dolls and dresses. The boy whose inherent empathy should have been appreciated and rewarded will probably learn to be tough, to stand up for himself, and not to take any guff from anyone. After a while, the boy and the girl will no longer even remember those childish (?) interests.

But you can't destroy inborn abilities. They just get pushed underground, into the unconscious. There an interesting thing takes place: those personality traits inevitably become personified. That is, a personality (or multiple personalities) form around the abilities that we diverted into the unconscious. Jung called this personality the Shadow because, like our physical shadow, it presents a dark outline of our total being. There is no logical necessity for this personification to occur; we could very well be constructed so the abilities merely lie dormant, awaiting some call from life that reawakens them.

Some animals are seemingly solitary by nature; they don't appear to need the company of others of their species. Usually, this is because of evolutionary pressures. For example, the poor orangutan has evolved over time into a solitary creature, because it lives in a region where its food supply is spread over so wide an area that a band of orangutans cannot find enough food to sustain them within a day's walk.

However, we humans are more like our cousins the monkeys—gregarious by nature. Isolated from other humans, we tend to become something less than human. That's why solitary confinement is the most feared punishment in a prison. In Peter Freuchen's *Book of the Eskimos*,[4] he tells the story of two trappers who spent the long Alaskan winter together. One died while the winter was still young. The other couldn't bear to be alone, so he kept the body frozen in a sitting position, and propped him up at a table in their cabin at mealtimes. That way, he could pretend that he still had a companion.

All our relationships with the world seem to eventually take on the form of our relationships with friends or enemies. We relate to the people we see on TV, the people we hear on the radio, as if they were intimate friends or relatives. Our pets become people to us. Even objects, like cars and computers, become personified if we like them enough. For example, one of the many charms of the columns Jerry Pournelle writes in computer magazines like *Byte* and *Infoworld* is that he has a name for each computer. These include his first computer: a Z80 (that's a computer chip for those who don't know) he calls Ezekial; its successor Zeke-II; his current mainstay: Big Cheetah; and his Cambridge Z88 laptop computer: Sir Zed. Even Jerry's home has a name—Chaos Manor.

---

[4]Peter Freuchen, *Book of the Eskimos* (Cleveland, OH: The World Publishing Company, 1961), pp. 344–361.

Similarly, a woman I know named every art object in her home that had any sort of human or animal appearance. There's Jeepers, the telephone stand that looks like a butler; Guillermo, the metal toucan; Alexander, the wooden rabbit; Hazel-Matilda, the stuffed witch, etc. It gives her a homey feeling just to come into the house and see all her friends.

THE SHADOW IN DREAMS

Inevitably we see the world through the lens of human relationships. Not surprisingly, our dreams are almost entirely about relationships with others. They're largely filled with the same people whom we have contact with in our day-to-day lives. But they're also populated with people who we know casually, if at all. And, from time to time, people appear whom we have never seen before (and probably never will): people created by the unconscious.

Jung felt that the qualities we have denied in our life don't go away, they are just relegated to the unconscious, where they become personified as the Shadow. When our conscious resources are inadequate to deal with some new issue in our life, and we need qualities that have been relegated to the unconscious from denial or neglect, those qualities show up as a Shadow figure in our dreams. Whenever we have Shadow dreams, we should view them as the beginning of some new life cycle. Because our lives are complex, at any one time in our lives, many such cycles of varying length are going on.

Shadow figures usually appear first as non-human: aliens from another planet, vampires, zombies, half-animal/half-human creatures, etc. They confront us with their unwanted, though unavoidable, presence. Over time, these dream figures evolve and become fully human, of the

Figure 9.   Shadow Dance. When we are finally forced to acknowledge the reality of the Shadow, at first our relationship is like an uneasy ritual dance, which is always threatening to deteriorate into active war. (Reprinted from *1001 Spot Illustrations of the Lively Twenties*.)

same sex as ourselves, but villainous, evil, despicable. (Certainly nothing like ourselves, perfect creatures that we are!) Later, they evolve still further into pitiful people whom we tolerate, but look down on, then into acquaintances— people whom we view as not particularly significant figures—but whom we tolerate as part of our everyday lives. Still later, the Shadow figures evolve into friends, relatives, lovers. Finally, if we have learned to integrate their unwanted character traits into our personality, they no longer have to be personified in the unconscious. We have changed and they are part of us.

Let me take that progression a bit more slowly with the little girl of my previous example. By the time she has become an adult, she will undoubtedly have long since quit trying to make use of her inborn mechanical abilities. For a time, her life may seem full and complete to her. But eventually something goes wrong. Perhaps she encounters a moral dilemma that she can't resolve with any of her normal rational resources. Or, perhaps, she finds herself inexplicably depressed, unable to work up an interest in anything. Try as she might to find a way to resolve her dilemma, or to break out of her depression, nothing helps.

That's because what she needs is in the unconscious, unavailable to her through her consciousness. When that time comes, the unconscious will begin to present her conscious awareness with Shadow figures formed around the personality traits that she has denied for all these years. At first, the Shadow figures in her dreams will probably be inhuman, and it will be impossible to identify the traits they possess. This marks a stage when the woman's conscious mind is being confronted with the need to develop abilities that she has denied as being possible for her. Therefore, the very idea will seem loathsome — inhuman.

Frequently, the denial will be so complete that Shadow dreams become nightmares. I've formed a habit that whenever I have a nightmare, I try to fall asleep again and go back into the nightmare in order to make peace with the nightmare figure. Sometimes this actually happens. More often, the attempt is enough to form some rapprochement between consciousness and the unconscious, and there is no further need for a nightmare.

The dream world provides a wonderful stage where many different situations can be played out, involving many different characters, leading to many different conclusions. People who claim they never dream would be shocked to discover the scenes that are played out in their psyches every night. In their dreams, they are confronted with exactly the situations they need to be confronted with in order to grow and develop. An evolution of character takes place slowly despite their lack of conscious awareness.

I've discussed the Shadow in the broader sense—in which the Shadow can appear as anyone from a dreaded nightmare figure to a friend or a relative—Shadow figures occur in dreams virtually every night. However, the extreme Shadow figures, that seem so loathsome to us, only appear when something has gone wrong with this process. Such Shadow figures show up when we have become too rigidly set in our ways. Think about the physical shadow. It only appears when light shines on us. The brighter the light, the darker the shadow. Similarly, if we see ourselves as too good, too perfect, the Shadow becomes darker in compensation.

THE PERSONA AND ITS RELATIONSHIP TO THE SHADOW

Jung called the face that we present to the world our "Persona," referring to the masks which the Greeks wore in their tragedies. However, the use of such symbolic characters is hardly limited to Greek drama. For example, the Japanese have similar masks which they use in their Noh drama. Each mask represents a fixed character type. The Balinese use similar symbolic figures in their puppet plays. The Punch and Judy figures, with their unchanging characters, are perennial favorites of British children. And, though they didn't wear masks, heroes and villains in American Westerns were (until the day of the anti-hero) similarly fixed character types. We all recognized the evil land-owner, the cold-blooded hired killer, the innocent damsel in distress, the alcoholic doctor, the tough barmaid with a heart of gold, the pure-as-the-driven-snow hero, and so on.

In the Western world in the late days of the 20th century, a man's occupation can frequently become his persona; that is, a man becomes an engineer or a computer programmer to such an extent that he forgets he is more than his job. Until recently, women had little or no opportunity for any adult roles other than "mother," "old maid," "school marm," "librarian," etc. Every woman who marries and has children knows how difficult it is to get other people to see her as a person in her own right, as someone other than her husband's wife, or her children's mother. She, herself, frequently has a hard time imagining herself except in those strongly archetypal roles.

We all need an identity and, rather than struggle to define our own unique identity, most of us are willing to take on a collective identity like "mother" or "father," "librarian" or "computer programmer." But those roles are like masks which can't change expressions. No matter what the situation, we have to react within our predefined character. When people are stuck in their persona, they appear shallow to us. They don't arouse much interest because they quite literally lack depth.

Similarly, we build up an ideal view of ourselves—kind and gentle, yet strong and forceful. (Or, trustworthy, loyal, helpful, brave, clean and reverent as the Boy Scouts would have it.) Any such picture composed exclusively of what we regard as good and right is too light; it lacks the dark shading required for completion. For example, in Britain in the latter half of the 19th century, the masculine ideal was the gentleman, with his exquisite self-mastery. The complement of that ideal was a savage, who was unable to control his instinctual drives. Of course, both these images existed only in the British mind, not in reality.

Under the illusion that they were in total control of their lives, the British upper class was in fact dominated by their unconscious. Driven by a need to find the savage necessary for their completeness, British males pushed Colonialism to its extremes, dominating India and Africa and all the other places of the world where they imagined savages dwelling. The British colonialists set up house in each country and attempted to live exactly as if they were still in England. In the middle of Africa, the British gentlemen put on starched collars, read their daily *London Times* (which was probably six months old by the time it reached them), and had their tea. More than anything, these colonists feared their fellow companions, unable to resist the pull from the unconscious, had "gone native."

In order to develop the self-discipline necessary for such insanity, young British boys of the upper class were sent to schools where they were savagely (sic) beaten and frequently sexually molested, by both their teachers and their fellow students. Their need for the repressed darkness and savagery led them ineluctably to masochism and sadism. Unable to connect sexuality and love, because it required some diminution of their conscious role of dominance, they became homosexuals in quite extraordinary numbers.[5]

---

[5]In no way do I mean to imply that all homosexuality comes about from such repression. It appears that a fixed percentage (often estimated at 10–15 percent) of men and women in any culture are homosexual, apparently genetically predisposed toward homosexuality just as most are genetically predisposed for heterosexuality. But circumstances can also lead a person whose sexuality is more borderline into one or the other camp. In the case of the fin-de-siècle Britain, circumstances pushed many upper-class males into an unhappy homosexuality, unhappy because it was probably not intended by nature.

Or consider an even greater phenomenon—Christianity—and the Shadow it has left in many of us. In sharp contrast to the patriarchal Jewish maxim of "an eye for an eye, a tooth for a tooth," Christ presented the world with a new, softer, more feminine idea—"love thy neighbor as thyself." What Christ was really expressing was the knowledge that he was not truly separate from the people around him, that he saw something of himself in everyone with whom he came into contact. But such a realization requires self-knowledge, and self-knowledge comes only from a long struggle with ourselves and, especially, with our Shadow.

His followers chose to take the "golden rule" as just that—a rule to be followed, much like they had followed the ten commandments of the Jewish religion. It is easier to just say that we have to love our neighbor, regardless of whether we do or not, than it is to search into the parts of ourselves that we would prefer to leave in the dark. Similarly, in following Christ's ideal, it is much easier to see him as perfect, incapable of sin, than it is to see him as a man struggling successfully with the contradictory sides of his own nature. What else could Christ do except struggle, composed as he was equally of God and man? In following Christ's ideal, we need to struggle with reconciling our essential animal nature with our equally essential divine nature. We need to find the divinity in the instinctual, the instinctual in the divine.

Instead, Christianity developed an ideal of perfection, of light without darkness. Darkness is split off and attributed to Satan, rather than being seen as a necessary part of our nature. If there's light, there's inevitably darkness to compensate. Therefore, all the neglected and repressed parts of the personality gather around the Shadow and become associated with sin and evil.

PROJECTION

Jesus also taught that we should first look to the mote in our own eye rather than to the evil in our neighbor. Psychologists use the term *projection* to refer to this attribution of our own characteristics to others. It's important to realize that projection is an unconscious process over which we have no control. The goal is to gain enough consciousness that we no longer have to project our Shadow onto others.

If we are sexually repressed, a Shadow figure forms who gives way to every sexual impulse. The more we deny that we have any such evil desires, the more energy gathers around that Shadow. Eventually there is so much energy that we can no longer confine it to the unconscious. It comes shooting forth. Sometimes it possesses us and we do things we would prefer to forget about afterward: "Boy, was I drunk! I don't remember a thing."

Or we project the Shadow out onto someone around us. Projections aren't totally indiscriminate; there has to be some sort of "hook" for the Shadow to attach itself to. But if the energy is strong enough, the hook doesn't have to be very close. In our example, we might project our Shadow of savage lust out onto anyone who wasn't as repressed as we were about sexuality. Once the projection was in place, we would attribute all sorts of characteristics to that unfortunate person which had little or nothing to do with their actual personality.

That's why our dreams present us with Shadow figures. In dreams, we can engage with them in safety. In the unconscious, we can have our arguments, fight our battles, and slowly come to respect their point-of-view, gradually learn to become a little looser ourselves. But if we remain consciously too rigid to make any changes in our value system, the Shadow figures become more and more threatening and eventually are projected out onto other people in the world. Once projected, we are eventually forced to confront the Shadow, unfortunately at the expense of the person receiving the projection.

The fact that this process occurs is amazing. Evidently, something within us won't accept our one-sided view of life. Jung called this inner process the *transcendent function* (in that it "transcends" our normal functional approach to life). The transcendent function attempts to restore wholeness by bringing repressed or ignored aspects of the personality into consciousness. Seen in that light, the Shadow provides an opportunity to grow. If acknowledged and related to, we grow. If denied and repressed, the Shadow grows stronger until we have to acknowledge and relate to it. The psyche is attempting to make us grow, whether we like it or not.

THE GIRL WITH MECHANICAL ABILITY

Let's return to our example of the little girl with mechanical ability. Forced to turn away from her "masculine" mechanical skills, she probably developed a Persona that was excessively feminine. She couldn't admit any masculine traits in her personality, because some part of her knew just how much she would have liked to tinker with her car, or design bridges, or fiddle with a computer. So she was forced to condemn anything even vaguely part of the supposed masculine world as unfeminine and, therefore, repugnant to her.

Let's imagine that she married a "big, tough man" who liked to "wear the pants in the house." For a while, she simpered and cooed over what a big strong man he was, and thought she liked her life. Soon after marrying, she had a little girl, then two years later a little boy. Now, it is a decade later. She loves both her children, and still loves her husband (though she has recently found herself growing tired of constantly having to play up to his "superior" ability in everything of significance). She doesn't know what is wrong with her lately, but life seems to have lost its zest. She finds herself just going through the motions.

We who are outside looking in on this woman's life can readily see what her problem is—she's lost part of her soul. She's no more the person she thinks she is than she's the Queen of England. But she lost her Shadow so long ago, she doesn't even remember she had one. Thankfully, it's still alive in the unconscious. Perhaps one night she has a dream. She can't remember it, but the dream has a disquieting affect on her. She's moody all the next day.

A few nights later, she has a dream that she does remember. It's a nightmare where a woman is chasing her—a terrible hulking woman, with hairy, heavily-muscled forearms. She knows if this woman catches her, she will crush her because the woman is as strong as a gorilla. She wakes in a cold sweat.

Later that week she thinks she sees the woman in the supermarket. When she looks closer, she can't imagine why she thought it was the woman from her dream. This woman was dark and had hair on her arms, but otherwise looked nothing like the woman in the dream. Later in the day, she sees an old "I Love Lucy" episode where Lucy and Ethel are trying to build a barbecue pit in the middle of the night. She laughs but, for a minute, finds herself thinking about how she would have built the barbecue pit. The thought passes so quickly that she doesn't even remember having it.

Well, I won't take you through all the stages. It might take a very long time. Usually, there would be some moment when the woman would cross her personal Rubicon. Most probably this would surface in some very slight action that she would not notice at the time. Perhaps one day, she just couldn't stand a dripping faucet one second longer. She had nagged her husband about it for weeks, but he'd ignored it. So she grabs a wrench and a washer and fixes it herself, without even realizing she knows how to fix it. She doesn't mention it to her husband. In fact, she tries to forget the incident entirely, because it makes her feel uneasy. But, from that moment on, her course is set.

Perhaps the reader might argue that the situation is too simple, life is more complex than any such easy summary. Granting that, consider that even this example is far from simple. This woman isn't going to change and become Josephine the plumber. She isn't going to lose the femininity she prizes so much. However, she might end up losing her husband. She is probably married to a weak man, because a strong man would have expected a real woman, and she didn't yet know what kind of woman she was when they married. As she regains her essential nature, she will gather strength. With her renewed strength, she'll appear strange and even frightening to her husband. Confrontations will occur.

It isn't easy to face the Shadow. It requires courage and, inevitably changes our lives! In order to recognize the Shadow, we have to recognize our projections, then remove them one at a time. That leads to the realization that we are each of us many people; that we are, at least in part, one with those around us. At the stage of the Shadow, that realization is only partial, but the path we follow afterward is ineluctable.

In this next section, I'll deal with the relationship between evil and the Shadow, and discuss some practical techniques for integrating the necessary qualities of the Shadow into our own personality.

THE SHADOW AND THE PROBLEM OF EVIL

> . . . the living form needs deep shadow if it is to appear plastic. Without shadow it remains a two-dimensional phantom, a more or less well brought-up child.[6]

When people first hear of Jung's concept of the Shadow, they usually envision something like "the dark force" in the "Star Wars" movies. They think of a struggle between light and dark, good and evil. Remember our discussion of how Christianity, with its goal of perfection, has far too frequently led to just such dichotomies, not only within each individual, but also within the entire Christian culture. If everything good is attributed to Christ and everything evil to Satan, there is no room for any shadings or ambiguity: Christians are good and everyone else is bad. The history of Christianity's pogroms against the Jews are sufficient evidence of the results of such a belief.

But, of course, Christianity is hardly alone. Islam, for example, has an identical split of darkness and light, good and evil, built into its religious dogma. In the Middle Ages, with Christianity and Islam equally convinced of moral rectitude, we had three hundred years of the nine bloody wars we call the Crusades. Can there be many episodes in history more reprehensible than the so-called Children's Crusade when thousands of children marched off to serve Christ, and ended up sold into slavery?

History reverberates with the calls of the morally righteous—Juan de Torquemada leading the Spanish Inquisition, Cotton Mather aiding and abetting the Salem witch trials. More recently, Jimmy Jones and the Guyana mass suicide, Khomeini and his fanaticism. The list is end-

---

[6]Carl Jung, *Collected Works*, Vol. 7, 400.

less. As soon as light is split off from darkness, and we identify ourselves exclusively with the light, everyone different from us becomes identified with the dark. But we need the values hidden in the dark just as we need the values openly acknowledged in the light. That need leads us to project the hidden darkness onto those we perceive as different from us. When the darkness comes to the surface, it brings with it associations to everything we have condemned to the darkness. We look at our enemies and see everything we don't want to see in ourselves. No wonder we try and destroy them with such ferocity.

It would seem that a tragedy as enormous as the Holocaust would have awakened us forever to the darkness that lies within us. Hitler's hate was built upon a vision of blonde Aryan supermen, married to blonde Aryan supermothers, breeding blonde Aryan superchildren. Darkness was projected out on everyone who didn't fit that image—

Figure 10.   Devilish Shadow. As long as we can remain unconscious of the Shadow as part of our personality, it is mixed with everything evil and devilish. (From *Le Chemin des Écoliers*. Reprinted from *Dore's Spot Illustrations*.)

African blacks, Orientals, gypsies, Eastern European peasants and, especially, the Jews.

But World War II was hardly over before Stalin built the Gulags and began the systematic extermination of an even greater number of people than died in the Holocaust. And the story goes on and on—Pol Pot murdered nearly the entire population of Cambodia; Idi Amin for a time stood in everyone's mind as the absolute leader of depravity. The systematic torture of political opponents is still occurring in El Salvador, in Guatemala, in Brazil, in fact, until recently in nearly every country of Latin and South America. In America, the hate-mongers have always waved the flag and preached Christian purity as they pour forth their venom against the traditional enemies, the Shadow people—the blacks and the Orientals and the Mexicans and the Puerto Ricans and the Jews.

The Shadow has to be dealt with, both in our individual lives and in the life of the culture we live in. It is the first stage toward consciousness. Without consciousness, we are at the mercy of the worst that lies within us. And that way leads to atrocities like those I've mentioned above, and many more too numerous to name.

THE SHADOW HIDDEN
WITHIN THE LIGHT OF SCIENCE

Let me tell a little story about evil. It's a story that's taught in college psychology classes, but there it's taught without any moral judgment, for moral judgments are not considered the province of science. The story is about John B. Watson, the founder of the prevailing psychology in America—behaviorism. Watson was fond of saying that if you gave him a child young enough, he could make him anything you wanted—a scientist, a lawyer, a criminal.

As proof, he once conducted a famous experiment on an 11-month-old boy named Albert. Watson coupled a frightening noise with the sight of a rat until the poor baby was terrified of rats. Then Watson "generalized" the association until Albert was frightened of all sorts of things—dogs, wool, furry objects, a Santa Claus mask. Watson had intended to see if he could then remove the fear by similar techniques. Unfortunately, Albert's mother, a worker at the hospital, left the hospital and Albert was left with his fears untreated.

In this case, the "light" was science, the "darkness" ignorance. Anything that increased the light was good, no matter what was required. Let me give another example from psychology—the famous experiments conducted by experimental psychologist Stanley Milgram in the early 1960s. When Milgram began these experiments, he actually hoped to prove that Germans were different from you and me, and that, therefore, the Holocaust couldn't happen here in America. He was planning to first conduct his research in America, then go to Germany for the second stage of the experiment. He never got beyond the first stage.

Milgram asked an experimental subject to help him with a learning experiment on another person who was supposedly the actual subject. That second subject was supposed to select the word that best associated with another word from a list of four or five words. If he picked the wrong word, he was given a small shock to encourage him to get it right the next time. If he missed again, the voltage of the shock was increased.

The experiment presented was actually a phony. There was no shock given to the supposed second subject; in fact, the second subject was another psychologist who was in on the experiment all along. The real point of the experiment was to see just how far the actual first subject would be willing to go in giving the electric shocks to the other person. The real subject had to administer the test, turn a dial to set the amount of the shock, then push a button to give the shock. The machine had a dial that was labelled all the way from "slight shock" to "danger: severe shock." Past that point were unlabelled points supposedly beyond the bounds of the test.

Milgram wanted to find out just how far people would go before they would refuse to administer any more shocks. Neither he nor any of his colleagues expected very many people would go on to the end. They were wrong. Every subject did! Milgram was startled and redesigned the experiment, making it more and more macabre in the process. He made a tape beforehand of the supposed subject crying out, begging for help, screaming, and at the end of the test, totally silent as if he had passed out. Still 65 percent of the subjects proceeded on to the end of the test!

The subjects didn't just blithely push the buttons. As the test went on, they reacted as any human being would. They begged Milgram to let them stop. He coldly told them to go on. They pleaded that the subject was dying. Milgram repeated that the subject was safe and the experiment must continue. That was the key phrase: "The experiment must continue."

Astonishingly, Milgram never did realize that he had placed himself in exactly the same relationship to the people administering the shock as they were to the subject who was supposedly being strapped in and receiving the shock. Milgram insisted that if he had been one of the subjects, he would have stopped. Yet, in effect, he was— and he didn't stop.

His manipulation of his subjects, lying to them from the beginning, was bad enough. But, at the start of his experiment, he never thought that it would lead to such terrifying results, such potentially damaging psychological results for his subjects. However, after the first experiments, when he found that it did, his humanity should have made him stop. But it didn't; the experiment had to continue.

Milgram never did admit that he was at fault. Many psychologists were appalled at the experiment. But, frighteningly, many more psychologists thought it was a grand idea and started designing similar experiments of their own based on tricking the subject. They argued: what a chance to get some real data; don't let the subject know he is a subject and you will get true responses. The morality of the situation was lost in the rush for more data. There has since been so much experimentation of this kind that one wonders if it is any longer possible to find a subject who will believe a psychological experimenter. After all, isn't it a given that the experimenter might lie to you? But all in the interests of science, you understand.

C. P. Snow considered the limits of the scientific attitude of detachment in his novel, *The Sleep of Reason.*[7] In this novel, two middle-aged women friends, perhaps lovers, are put on trial for torturing a small boy. They did so largely out of curiosity, and with a dispassionate, clinical quality that would not have been out of place in a research laboratory. In the course of the trial, all our normal attempts to distance ourselves from such actions are confounded. It becomes clear that, within any normal definition of sanity, the two women are perfectly sane. It also seems likely that the event, having been committed, would never be repeated. Though their act was monstrous, they are not monsters. We can't find any line which will separate them from us. As the trial went on, the reader was forced more and more to the conclusion reached by the 19th-century barrister, who, after having condemned a man to death, said, "There but for the grace

---

[7]C. P. Snow, *The Sleep of Reason* (New York: Charles Scribner's Sons, 1968).

of God, go I." Or, as Albert the Alligator says in "Pogo," "We has seen the enemy and he is us."

We are all afraid of looking at the monsters that we fear lie within us. The ancient story of Pandora's Box counsels us to leave hidden things unexamined. Yet it is precisely when we don't examine our hidden side that it builds to monster proportions, and comes bursting forth into the outer world. Once we begin to acknowledge that the monsters we see without, live within, that danger is abated. Instead we find the beginnings of the wisdom that every supposed monster can teach us.

Perhaps we can understand Milgram's subjects; we can even understand Milgram, himself. If we stretch ourselves, we can put ourselves in John B. Watson's shoes. And that's a first step, which we need so desperately, at integrating the Shadow.

WORKING WITH
THE SHADOW IN YOUR DREAMS

When you find yourself in conflict with someone else in a dream, assume that the other person is a Shadow figure who possesses some quality that you need to integrate into your personality. Making this assumption is correct nearly all the time in dreams. The times when you are truly in the right and the dream is accurately summarizing the situation are infrequent enough that you can consider them the exceptions that prove the rule.

The more intense the struggle, the more sure you can be that you're dealing with a Shadow figure. Similarly, the more repugnant or disagreeable you find the other person, the more likely that this is a Shadow figure. At first, this is hard to acknowledge, since Shadow figures invariably represent qualities that we refuse to admit are part of our own personality. But once you accept this premise, you will come to regard Shadow dreams as presenting opportunities for advancement rather than merely disagreeable, nightmarish interludes.

If you consciously accept that you are dealing with a Shadow part of your own personality, you will find that over time your dreams display the evolution of the Shadow that I mentioned earlier (from inhuman, to despised human, to tolerated human). Invariably, there is also an evolution from vague and amorphous to more sharply defined. This is because, as your consciousness engages with the unconscious, the definition of your particular Shadow will become more precise. When you are dealing with a part of your personality that you have previously rejected, you are hardly in a position to make fine shadings of value when you first encounter the Shadow. Later, you will come to discover what your unique unconscious abilities actually are.

Don't worry if, during this process of confronting the Shadow, you fail to consciously understand what it represents. Just keep honoring it by admitting to yourself that the Shadow is probably right and you're probably wrong. Most often, the issue will resolve itself long before you are able to consciously understand what the issue was.

For example, a patient had a dream where a cheap, greedy black man owned a hotel where he and his wife were staying. The black man had constructed the bathrooms so that anyone who wanted to use them had to go through a complicated two-step procedure, paying for each stage. At the time, he only partially understood the dream's message: he realized it indicated that he needed some characteristics that he regarded as "greedy," but he didn't know what those characteristics were.

In actuality, he was entering a time in his life when he needed to think less about others and more about himself, because he was preparing to make a major career change. He had so many people who were dependent on him for emotional support that he didn't have time to sort out his own difficulties. Only later did he realize that the Shadow figure was telling him that he needed to make it more difficult for others to "dump their crap" on him. Though, of course, he wasn't able to sort all that out at the time when he had this dream, he did at least recognize that it was a Shadow dream and that he probably needed to be willing to be more "greedy."

The choice of a "black man" is a typical choice of the unconscious for a white male dreamer. Having such a dream doesn't mean that the dreamer is a bigot. Typical Shadow dreams of Caucasians use black men, Native Americans, Indians (from India), Mexican peasants, etc. to represent Shadow elements. Black men are likely to use white men for their Shadow—plus most of the combinations mentioned previously, except black men, of course. In other words, our dreams use people from whatever race or nationality most different to our own experience to represent the Shadow.

When Shadow issues are coming close to resolution, there is frequently an ambiguity of identity in a dream, especially ambiguity between yourself and some other figure. For example, a middle-aged female patient had a series of dreams where it wasn't clear to her if she was in the dream herself, or whether it was some young woman quite a bit younger than the patient's actual age. The dream symbolism indicates that a merger of the middle-aged woman and a younger part of herself was close to occurring.

SPOTTING THE SHADOW IN EVERYDAY LIFE

Learning to recognize the Shadow in your dreams helps you recognize the Shadow in everyday life. Look for emotional outbursts. If someone really gets on your nerves, he or she is likely to be "carrying your Shadow" for you; you are projecting your Shadow onto someone who provides a hook for it. In those cases, rather than stay with the emotion, try and tell yourself that it is your issue, not his or hers, and that you are projecting the Shadow.

This is much more difficult to accept in everyday life than it is with dream figures. Even when you consciously understand the process of projecting the Shadow, you will find yourself denying that you're doing it. You will keep saying some variety of "yes, but" to yourself. The angrier the person makes you, the more sure you can be that you're encountering your Shadow. Shadow anger will have an unreasoning quality about it which you can gradually distinguish from the righteous anger you experience over a true injustice. Again it's best in the early stages of dealing with Shadow issues to always assume that it is your issue, not the other person's. You won't be wrong very often if you make that assumption.

Gradually you will progress in dealing with Shadow projections. At first, you will only be able to recognize the projection after the fact. Don't be discouraged; that's the first step toward removing the projection and integrating the Shadow. Later, you will find that you can recognize the projection in real time. That is, you get angry, blow up, then immediately realize that you're projecting. Still later, you recognize your anger before it comes out and, consequently, you don't have to express it.

Once you get better at the process, there will nearly always be an inner pause between an event that triggers anger and the expression of the anger. You can then choose to express the anger because it is appropriate or suppress it because it is inappropriate. This conscious suppression of anger is far different than unconsciously repressing anger because you are afraid to deal with it. Projection is an unconscious process; once you become aware of your own projections, they gradually cease.

Shadow figures then move to your dreams where you can deal with them more effectively than you can in your everyday life.

Because we are continually excavating forgotten parts of our personality from the unconscious which we need at a particular stage of our development, we continue to have Shadow dreams throughout our life. However, there is a distinct Shadow stage in the individuation process. That is, once consciousness engages with the unconscious in order to accelerate the process of individuation, we will typically encounter Shadow issues. We will also encounter issues with the Anima and Animus, with the Self, or with the Mother and Father complex—archetypes that we will discuss in later chapters. However, usually the overwhelming scope of the issues in the early stage of this process involves the Shadow.

The Shadow stage is that stage of our development where we are forced to consciously admit that some unwanted personality traits are part of us. Once we have gone through this process fully, we have passed a distinct stage in our own personal development. Though we will have other Shadow figures appear in the future, we will never again have to learn the process of integrating the Shadow. Once the Shadow is integrated, we pass on to the next archetype, which Jung called the Anima/Animus.

CHAPTER 6

THE ANIMA AND ANIMUS

Every man carries within him the eternal image of woman, not the image of this or that particular woman, but a definite feminine image. . . . The same is true of the woman: she too has her inborn image of man.
— Carl Jung

The Anima (Latin for Soul) is the feminine aspect of a man's unconscious, the Animus (Latin for mind or spirit) the masculine aspect of a woman's unconscious. Integrating the Anima or Animus is a much more difficult task than integrating the Shadow.

Integrating the Shadow requires a high level of courage and honesty, but this is only the first step toward psychological and spiritual growth. Accepting the Shadow as part of our personality requires us to redefine who we are and what we believe. We have to acknowledge that we do, in fact, have needs and desires that we previously considered worthless or immoral. That new self-definition then inevitably forces a new set of moral choices upon us. Before we accepted the Shadow, many actions were unthinkable because we "just weren't that kind of person." Now our horizons are broadened, and we find that situations we previously saw as either black or white, now appear gray. Consequently, the transition from the Shadow stage to the stage of the Anima and Animus is frequently marked by some action on our part that will ultimately lead us to deep emotional turmoil.

HOW JUNG DEVELOPED THE CONCEPT OF THE ANIMA/ANIMUS

Jung's concept of the Anima/Animus is often criticized today as sexist. It's important to realize that Jung was pioneering women's rights. At a time when women's values were largely ignored, Jung argued that a man had to come to grips with his feminine qualities, and a woman with her masculine qualities, in order to become a whole person. This was, and still is, a radical idea. Unfortunately, in his descriptions of the Anima and the Animus, Jung frequently took for granted the universality of the masculine and feminine personality traits of his day. This is particularly offensive to many women, since the last thing women need today is a theory that predefines what women are and are not capable of.

We are just beginning to think deeply about the similarities and differences between men and women. At this early stage of our investigation, no one knows with certainty just which abilities and personality traits are culturally imposed on men and women, and which are inborn. Like all nature/nurture issues, the situation is complex and doesn't lend itself to easy generalizations. However, it is clear that men have artificially limited the social possibilities for women in virtually all cultures. Modern women are demonstrating that they can do anything a man can do if given the opportunity.

TROILUS AND CRISEYDE. LIBER SECUNDUS.

Figure 11. In dealing with the animus and anima, we are often forced to choose between those values we hold most dear—much as in the *Iliad*, when Cressida found herself pulled between the "undying love" she had felt for Troilus and the new love she felt for Diomedes. (*Troilus and Criseyde.* Reprinted from *William Morris: Ornamentation & Illustrations from the Kelmscott Chaucer.*)

As with virtually all his discoveries, Jung came to his concept of the Anima/Animus originally by necessity, and developed it over time as his knowledge of it grew. As you will remember from chapter 4, this was the identical pattern Jung followed in developing his theory of psychological types. Jung at first thought that it was enough to separate people into introverts, who experienced the world subjectively, and extraverts, whose experience of the world was objective. He thought that introverts primarily thought things through, while extraverts responded to the people and objects of the world through feeling. Gradually he came to realize that thinking and feeling (and later sensation and intuition) were independent dimensions of personality, which could be either introverted or extraverted.

Similarly, Jung's initial concept of the Shadow as the "other" who carries our repressed or undeveloped characteristics was mixed up with the concept of the Shadow as the archetypal figure personifying evil. Since the Shadow, like any cognitive invariant, is collective, we can never reach an end to it. Once we integrate all our ignored personal Shadow qualities, there still remain qualities that are so alien to us that we will never integrate them into our personality. In the unconscious they will necessarily be associated with evil since they are so far outside our experience. But this isn't to say that the Shadow is evil, not even the collective Shadow that remains after we have integrated our personal Shadow qualities. It just means that the relationship between conscious and unconscious is too complex to be easily put into categories.

Jung continued to worry over the concept of evil throughout his long working life, and was still writing about it in his last works. Though it is clear from his writing that he was well aware of all that I have said above, he never makes this separation as clear as he does with psychological types. Unfortunately the concept of the Anima/ Animus suffers from the same lack of clear discrimination.

Jung first developed the concept of the Anima/ Animus at the same time as his theory of psychological types. At the end of *Psychological Types*,[1] Jung included 80 pages of definitions. Each definition was a wonderful mini-essay which capsulized Jung's ideas at this early stage of thought. The definition in question is not called

---

[1]Carl Jung, *Collected Works*, Vol. 6.

Anima or Animus, but soul. Jung argued that we all contain an autonomous personality, which structures our inner life, and is projected out onto the world. This personality is what men and women throughout the ages have called the soul.

Jung soon realized that he needed to find a neutral term which didn't have the religious overtones (especially Christian) that soul had acquired over the years. The religious concept of the soul has a very long history, going back to India nearly three thousand years ago. Over the course of the millennia since, it acquired a penumbra of doctrinal overlays specific to the cultures in which it evolved. For example, as taught in modern Christianity, the soul is the eternal portion of a person, which inhabits the body while we live, then leaves the body at death. This is not what Jung meant by the term. It would have been a hopeless task for Jung to ask modern men and women to set aside everything they had learned about the soul in growing up, in order to return to their own personal experience. So he needed a new term.

Jung's vast knowledge of dreams, myths, and fairy tales convinced him that men experienced their soul as feminine, women as masculine; therefore, he decided to use the Latin terms *Anima* and *Animus* as substitutes for soul. In his mini-essay on soul in *Psychological Types*, this concept was still so new that he only used the word Anima twice and Animus once. But once he arrived at these terms, he used them exclusively throughout the remainder of his life and never returned to the concept of soul.[2]

---

[2]For those interested in exploring the history of the concept of soul, I can highly recommend John A. Sanford's *Soul Journey: A Jungian Analyst Looks at Reincarnation* (New York: Crossroad Publishing Company, 1991).

TWO ASPECTS TO THE ANIMA/ANIMUS

As we discussed at length in the previous material on the Shadow, when life becomes too one-sided, when we have exhausted our conscious resources, we are forced to turn to the unconscious. In the unconscious, the very personality traits that we need become personified as the Shadow. Whether encountered in our dreams or projected out onto others in the world, eventually our consciousness is forced to confront those Shadow qualities. As we come to deal more honestly with the fact that we possess such qualities, the Shadow figures evolve in the unconscious. Eventually, these needed qualities become so integrated into the personality that they are a part of us. At that point, Anima/Animus issues appear in our life.

That is the chain of events as normally presented in Jungian psychology. It is reasonably close to reality, but it needs some emendation. In actuality, once we have integrated the personal aspects of the Shadow into the personality, two separate issues appear, which are confused because both are represented in our dreams (and in projections out onto the world) by figures of the opposite sex:

1) *further personal Shadow issues* that are disguised because the Shadow is now represented by a person of the opposite sex. Then, as those qualities are integrated into the personality, we encounter a true cognitive invariant;

2) an *impersonal, collective archetype of relationship* between us and the world, whether inner or outer, which is what Jung meant by the Anima/Animus. This is represented by the opposite sex because our relationship with the opposite sex is the primary relationship in our adult lives.

What I'm terming the Shadow characteristics of the Anima/Animus, Jung discussed as the unconscious contents of the Anima/Animus which could be integrated into consciousness. When he was referring to the Anima/Animus as the archetypal representation of relationship, Jung described it as the *function* with which we relate to the collective unconscious, in the same way as we relate to the outer world through the Persona.

But before we explore the archetypal aspect of the Anima/Animus as the impersonal function of relationship through which the world is filtered, let's discuss the simpler issue—the Shadow aspect of the Anima/Animus.

THE ANIMA/ANIMUS AS SHADOW

Whether or not we human beings innately possess abilities and traits based strictly upon our gender, culture has forced such a separation of abilities upon us. Until very recently, the roles of men and women have been sharply divided. Because of that separation over millennia, certain ways of relating to the world have come to be represented in the unconscious by women, others by men. We encountered a similar situation previously with the Shadow. Shadow issues are represented in the dreams of a Caucasian by blacks or Indians, etc. (and, of course, Caucasians represent the Shadow for blacks, etc.) regardless of the dreamer's bigotry or lack of bigotry. The unconscious is a natural force like the ocean or the winds; like those natural forces, the unconscious is immune to our moral judgments.[3]

We are not all born with identical abilities and needs, as we mentioned in our discussion of psychological types.

---

[3]This is an excellent reason why the unconscious, as represented in dreams, should not be blindly obeyed.

Jung identified some of those differences (extraversion and introversion, thinking, feeling, sensation, and intuition) as separate psychological functions. We each concentrate on our strengths (those abilities contained within our dominant function) until they are highly developed (thinking, for example). Then we concentrate on developing one or both of our auxiliary functions. (In this example, those would be sensation and intuition.) We'll probably never fully develop these auxiliary functions, certainly not to the extent of our dominant function, but we can go a long way.

The inferior function (feeling, in this case) is another story, however. As we have seen in our discussion of the Shadow, we finally reach a point when we can no longer do without the inferior function. That's because it is the only door to the numinous experience of the collective unconscious. It is this search for the numinous that forces us eventually to encounter the Shadow.

Once we have dealt successfully with all the parts of our inferior function (represented by someone of the same sex), the unconscious has to turn to figures of the opposite sex. It doesn't have any other possibilities. Now that wouldn't necessarily be so in a culture where there was little separation of roles between men and women. Our dreams could continue to use same-sex figures, and the ambiguity I'm discussing wouldn't exist. Of course, it is also quite likely that, in such a culture, the Shadow wouldn't necessarily be a person of the same sex as the dreamer. The traditional Jungian formula of same sex = Shadow, opposite sex = Anima/Animus would cease to be relevant. But we don't live in such a culture, and as far as can be determined at this point in the scholarship on gender, no such culture has existed to date.

> . . . if, as the result of a long and thorough analysis
> and the withdrawal of projections, the ego has

been successfully separated from the unconscious, the anima will gradually cease to act as an autonomous personality and will become a function of relationship between conscious and unconscious.[4]

Separating these contra-sexual Shadow figures from figures representing the Anima/Animus as an impersonal function is far from easy, and is largely unaddressed by Jung. This is enough of a problem that there is a temptation to throw out Jung's model of the Anima/Animus entirely, but that would be throwing out the baby with the bath water. It does seem to be true that we structure reality through a cognitive invariant, which does seem to personify in the unconscious as a figure of the opposite sex. It's just that not all such figures represent that function. Ah, life is hard, isn't it?

Happily, you can do much of the necessary psychological work without recognizing the distinction I've made at all. To the extent that a normal male in our culture actually becomes more sensitive and receptive (the normal needs for a Western male when he has exhausted the masculine Shadow), or a female more discriminating and assertive (normal needs for a Western female having integrated her feminine Shadow), they will both integrate the contra-sexual aspect of the Shadow and start to relate more consciously to the Anima/Animus.

The hard part, even in these more enlightened days, is for a man to acknowledge that a woman may have character traits that he needs and desires (and vice versa). But again, at the risk of being redundant, these traits are not necessarily fixed for men and women across all cultures and times. And even within our own culture, they fit some men and women strongly, some less so, and some almost not at all.

---

[4]Carl Jung, *Collected Works*, Vol. 16, 504.

The case is clearest for those members of each sex whose strengths and weaknesses are not considered normal in our culture for their sex. Remember the example of the little girl with repressed mechanical ability. She is very unlikely to find role models among other women; she is largely forced to look to men for those particular personality traits that only men possess in large numbers in our culture. Similarly, men have to stop asking, like Professor Higgins in *My Fair Lady*, "Why can't a woman be more like a man?" Men have to start asking, "How can a man be more like a woman?" (without ceasing to be a man).

The 1980s saw many short-lived attempts at solving this problem through androgyny: remember how exciting (and a little scary) Boy George initially seemed, with his makeup and feminine manner and dress? Or remember Grace Jones, with her appearance somewhere between Amazon and dominatrix. These images seem tame now and more than a little bit silly. Sexual androgyny isn't the goal; it is just an intermediate attempt to try on the characteristics we associate with the opposite sex for a time in order to discover what it feels like. Ultimately, men have to come back to being men, women to being women—within their cultures, but with a broader lens through which they can view reality.

THE ANIMA/ANIMUS AS THE ARCHETYPE OF RELATIONSHIP

. . . The anima is nothing but a representation of the personal nature of the autonomous system in question. What the nature of this system is in a transcendental sense, that is, beyond the bounds of experience, we cannot know.

I have defined the anima as a personification of the unconscious in general, and have taken it as a

Figure 12. In dealing with the anima and animus, the feeling is much like a tug of war with eros in between. (Reprinted from *1001 Spot Illustrations of the Lively Twenties*.)

bridge to the unconscious, in other words, as a function of relationship to the unconscious.[5]

After we have integrated the Shadow aspects of the Anima/Animus, what is left that is best represented in the unconscious by the opposite sex? The relationship! The relationship between a man and a woman, a totality which is bigger than either of the two individual participants in the relationship. This relationship is so significant in our lives that we filter much of our perception of reality, whether inner or outer reality, through that experience. The archetypal aspect of the Anima/Animus isn't governed by the particular characteristics the opposite sex possess; it's determined by the one relationship we all have with someone who is necessarily different than we are, yet not thereby seen like the Shadow, as an opponent.

---

[5]Carl Jung, *The Collected Works*, Vol. 13: *Alchemical Studies*, copyright © 1967 (Princeton: Princeton University Press), 61–62.

Just as introvert and extravert take their characteristic paths through the myriads of choices of life, so are our lives structured through the inborn sexual behaviors and archetypal structures that we evidence toward the opposite sex. That is, we behave toward the world much as we behave toward the opposite sex. If we tend to dominate our sexual partner, we tend to dominate other people and other situations. If we flirt, but don't commit with our sexual partners, we are likely to deal the same way with all that comes into our lives. That is exactly what the Anima/Animus is: an inner structure through which we filter nearly everything with which we have a relationship in life, because the primary adult relationship is that between man and woman.

Of course, the real-life situation is far more complex than that easy summary. There are many relationships in our lives other than those with the opposite sex—e.g., as a child, a boy's father, a girl's mother, friends, fellow students, teachers, and adult relationships with colleagues and bosses, etc. All these relationships provide filters through which life's experiences pass into our consciousness. However, with the exception of the childhood relationship with parents, none of those other relationships are likely to compare in strength and complexity with the relationship to the opposite sex.

As long as we have unresolved childhood issues with our parents, those issues continue to take center stage in our adult life. Once those childhood issues are resolved, our relationship with the opposite sex becomes the primary relationship in each of our adult lives. Frequently it is the very appearance of the opposite sex in our lives which forces us to finally resolve childhood issues. Any relationship strong enough to pull us away from the childhood attachment to parents is very strong indeed, and thereafter becomes the primary psychic filter.

THE EMOTIONAL TURMOIL
CAUSED BY THE ANIMA/ANIMUS

We must begin by overcoming our virtuousness, with the justifiable fear of falling into vice on the other side. This danger certainly exists, for the greatest virtuousness is always compensated inwardly by a strong tendency to vice, and how many vicious characters treasure inside themselves sugary virtues and a moral megalomania.[6]

All the stages of a man's experience of woman—mother, sister, lover, mate—are experiences of the outer world, experiences of the first half of life. Just as the Shadow arrives to awaken us to our inner needs as the second half of life begins, the Anima/Animus continues the inner work begun by the Shadow. I began this chapter by saying that entering the Anima/Animus stage was likely to lead us to emotional turmoil. The difference between the struggle during the Shadow stage and the struggle during the Anima/Animus stage is like the difference between admitting to ourselves that we desire someone else sexually and actually dealing with the changes that occur in our lives after we become sexually active. And that's a very profound difference, indeed.

In order to integrate the Shadow, we have to accept that we have thoughts and desires that don't fit our pristine image of ourselves. We have to accept that there is more to us than the role we play in society or in the home. We have to stop condemning those around us, withdraw our projections from those we condemn, and accept that the problem lies within us. And then, we have to stop condemning ourselves as well. We have to understand

---

[6]Jung quotation, in Jolande Jacobi and R. F. C. Hull, eds. *C. G. Jung: Psychological Reflections* (Princeton: Bollingen Series, Princeton University Press, 1973), p. 102.

that those seemingly awful qualities we try to run away from might have some meaning in our lives.

This requires enormous courage and honesty, and a great deal of patient work. However, most of the work we do in integrating the Shadow into the personality is work with the personal unconscious. At the core of the Shadow is a cognitive invariant of the feared "other" that transcends our personal experience and is, therefore, collective. But the qualities we integrate into the personality are our own (though sometimes "dis"-owned). Once we quit fighting against them, we can feel the force of recognition.

The Anima and Animus are quite different matters. In this next section, I'll discuss practical techniques for the integration of the Anima/Animus, and trace its more recent archetypal development.

ANIMA/ANIMUS IN OUR DREAMS

> . . . The world is empty only to him who does not know how to direct his libido towards things and people, and to render them alive and beautiful. What compels us to create a substitute from within ourselves is not an external lack, but our own inability to include anything outside ourselves in our love.[7]

The Anima and Animus appear in dreams in much more complex ways than with the Shadow. We now know that what appears to be the archetype of the Anima/Animus may actually be another stage of the Shadow, one necessarily represented by figures of the opposite sex. This is often clearly represented by a figure who combines the Shadow with the Anima/Animus (the Caucasian may see a dark-skinned figure of the opposite sex, etc.).

---

[7]Carl Jung, *Collected Works*, Vol. 5, 253.

If people have unresolved parent/child issues (and who doesn't?), the Anima/Animus is frequently mixed with the Mother or Father archetype in the early stages of dreams. One of the most common manifestations of this for a man is an attractive, dominant woman who he feels both attracted to and frightened of. If the man has not been able to successfully separate from his mother (and remember we are talking not only of his physical mother, but the mother archetype), the woman in his dreams may actually even devour him. Such dreams reflect the conflict between the desire for comfort and security (represented by the mother) versus the desire for passion and excitement (represented by a sexual partner). There are as many variations on this theme as there are men and women.

It is frequently said in Jungian literature that the Anima appears in a man's dreams as a succession of single well-defined women, and the Animus appears in a woman's dreams as groups of relatively undefined men. Though this is accepted fairly broadly, I have never found any support for this theory in examining my own dreams and the dreams of patients, friends, and acquaintances. I find that both men and women usually dream of single defined figures, though both sometimes dream of groups of undefined figures of the opposite sex. (By this time, I'm sure that readers recognize those groups of undefined figures as early Anima/Shadow figures.)

A person's mate, or significant other, appears in dreams far more often than any other figure of the opposite sex. Frequently, this person is just what he or she appears to be—the actual person. In those cases, the dream is presenting some conflict between the dreamer and the mate that needs to be resolved. But more often, the mate is still another representation of the contra-sexual qualities of the dreamer. After all, we are more likely to generalize about the opposite sex from what we know in the normal course of our life. In those cases, it is helpful to think of the mate as representing those qualities of the opposite sex that we feel we know and understand.

GODS AND GODDESSES IN OUR DREAMS

Frequently, the Anima/Animus appears in dreams as a god or a goddess. In our day and age, the closest thing we have to gods and goddesses are celebrities, so the celebrities we encounter in our dreams should be considered as modern-day gods and goddesses. So it becomes important to consider what a god or goddess represents.

Remember Jung's efforts to understand the temperamental differences between Freud and Adler, and between both and himself? This led him to realize that human beings fall into a finite number of different personality types. He then evolved his system of psychological types to explain those differences. Basically, this split people into pairs of opposites, based on a number of characteristics which Jung discovered to be basic to all human beings (introversion versus extraversion, thinking versus feeling, sensation versus intuition). This was similar to the way the ancient Greeks identified four basic personality types—humours—based on the polarities of hot versus cold, and dry versus wet.

However, there is an alternative way—equally ancient—to classify differences in personality. Rather than looking for underlying polarities, you identify particular types of people based on some predominant characteristic of personality which overshadows everything else, for example, "the miser" or "the seductress." The advantage of creating categories is that new categories can be added whenever another new type is identified. The disadvantage is that there is no systematic method that links all of the personality types; there can readily be a hundred personality types, or even a thousand. But, in practice, such categories are usually limited to a relatively small number of personalities.

In a wide variety of ancient cultures, each distinct personality trait valued by that culture was personified by a god or a goddess. For example, warlike strength was personified by the Roman god Mars, the Greek Ares, the Norse god Thor, etc. In the 1990s that strength is better embodied in movie personalities such as Sylvester Stallone or Arnold Schwarzenegger. In ancient times, clever and mischievous trickery was represented by the Roman Mercury, the Greek Hermes, the Norse Loki. In our times, perhaps Billie Crystal or Eddie Murphy more readily come to mind? For the Romans, Venus was the incarnation of love and beauty; for the Greeks, it was Aphrodite. More than any other modern celebrity, Marilyn Monroe represented that archetype, but contemporary female figures as widely different in character as Julia Roberts and Madonna compete in representing opposing aspects of Venus/Aphrodite.

Any trait that we admire, desire, or fear is likely to be projected out onto a god or goddess. When we still believed in a panoply of gods and goddesses, altars were built to honor them, and sacrifices were offered to curry their favor. The gods and goddesses in current favor were easily recognized by the number of people attending their shrines, and by the richness of the offerings on their altars. If a shrine was unattended and covered with weeds, you could be assured that the characteristics of that god or goddess were no longer highly valued or feared by their society. Today we can look to the box office receipts for an instant evaluation of which god or goddess is in or out of favor with mere mortals.

Every god or goddess who has ever lived still exists somewhere in the ancestral memories all humans possess. Humanity has not changed much over the one to two million years (depending on who is counting) of human

Figure 13. In mythology, each god or goddess largely stood for a single representative human trait, taken to more than human dimensions. For the Romans, Venus represented feminine beauty. Gods and goddesses still appear in our dreams and projections—though in modern times they are more likely to be movie stars or rock stars. (*Venus and Cupid*. Reprinted from *Pictorial Archive of Decorative Renaissance Woodcuts*.)

Figure 14.   To the Romans, Mars stood for masculine strength. Today Mars takes the form of Arnold Schwarzenegger or Sylvester Stallone. (*Mars*. Reprinted from *Pictorial Archive of Decorative Renaissance Woodcuts*.)

history. We have more in common with our relatives living in caves or on the African savannah than we have differences. A relatively small number of character traits appeared early in human history and have continued largely unchanged throughout the years. The history of the gods and goddesses is a history of the variations on those eternal human types (or if not strictly eternal, so slowly evolving that they seem so).

Though we may daydream about meeting a movie star or rock star (remember, they are the gods and goddesses of the present day), we would undoubtedly be petrified if such a meeting actually occurred. We endow them with such inhuman perfection that a real relationship would be impossible. But our dreams don't stop at that point: just as the ancient myths loved to present stories of gods and goddesses walking the earth, encountering normal people, our dreams bring us together with our current gods.

When we need to relate to the world in a new and different manner, our dreams produce a god or goddess who possesses the abilities we need. We oppose the Shadow because we don't want to change. We fall in love with a God or Goddess because it is everything we have ever wanted to possess. With the Shadow, we have to identify the traits it represents that we need. With the Anima/Animus we have to realize that we must not always look to another to give meaning to life. The Shadow evolves into more familiar figures until the Shadow and we are one. The Anima/Animus figure evolves into someone we can be comfortable with in a human way.

ANIMA/ANIMUS PROJECTIONS

When projected, the anima always has a feminine form with definite characteristics. This empirical finding does not mean that the archetype is constituted like that *in itself*. The male-female syzygy is only one among the possible pairs of opposites, albeit the most important one in practice and the commonest. . . . [A]n archetype in its quiescent, unprojected state has no exactly determinable form but is in itself an indefinite structure which can assume definite forms only in projection.[8]

Dealing with the Anima/Animus is much more difficult because the Anima/Animus is one step deeper into the collective unconscious. We are no longer dealing just with our own personal qualities, whether conscious or unconscious. Rather, we are dealing with *archetypal relationships between men and women*, which form an inner lens through which all relationships are viewed. When men and women fall in love, it is a shock to their system. All the rules fall away and they become totally possessed by the lover. Life only has meaning when they are with this lover, or at least thinking about the lover. That lover is perfection itself, beyond any reproach or criticism.

We have already learned enough about the nature of projection from dealing with the Shadow to realize that projections reveal more about ourselves than they do about the other person. No actual person is that wonderful, just as no actual person is as evil as our Shadow projections would have us believe. As with the Shadow, when we fall in love, we are projecting our inner contra-sexual qualities onto someone who provides a convenient "hook."

Later, as the relationship continues, lovers begin to see the real person, rather than the projection. That's frequently enough of a shock to terminate the relationship! Many people never go further than that in any relationship; they just fall in love serially, never deepening their involvement with the opposite sex and, therefore, never coming to recognize the contra-sexual parts of their own

---

[8]Carl Jung, *Collected Works*, Vol. 9, I, 142.

personality. We've all seen people who continue to make the same deadly mistakes in their sexual relationships, never learning from their mistakes, never recognizing the repetitive nature of their love affairs.

Fortunately, most of us do learn from our experiences. Adolescents date in order to learn about the opposite sex, and through that experience, learn about themselves. Our first loves can be driven by projection onto hooks so flimsy that afterward we can't recognize what it was that we thought we saw in the other person. A few years ago, I talked to a bright young woman about what she liked in a date. One requirement was that he own a red car. She said that turned her on. And I stress that this was a bright young woman.

Recently I read a newspaper article where a woman reporter discussed the changes in her life caused by dyeing her hair blonde. Suddenly virtually every male reacted to her in a strongly sexual way. Men with whom she already had a casual friendship became either sexually embarrassed or flirtatious. The blonde hair was enough to provide a hook for their Anima projections.

> . . . projection is an unconscious, automatic process whereby a content that is unconscious to the subject transfers itself to an object, so that it seems to belong to that object. The projection ceases the moment it becomes conscious, that is to say when it is seen as belonging to the subject.[9]

Just as with the Shadow, we need to stop projecting the Anima/Animus out onto people in the outer world, and instead accept that those characteristics are within ourselves. This can be more difficult with the Anima/Animus than with the Shadow. When we are projecting the Shadow out onto the world, we inevitably come into

---

[9]Carl Jung, *Collected Works*, Vol. 9, I, 121.

conflict, and that conflict is likely to eventually force all but the most stubborn of us into some examination of our values. The projection of the Anima/Animus can instead lead to a life where we continue to chase one love after another. Frequently this is literally a lover of the opposite sex, but also frequently the "lover" might be a succession of belief systems, or hobbies, or . . . ?

Hopefully, we eventually begin to realize that the successive failures of our relationships (whether with a person or a belief system, etc.) are our own fault, not the fault of a partner. Since both sides of the relationship are equally involved, it takes both to make the relationship work, but only one to destroy it. We have to discover how to resolve these issues both in the outer and inner life.

A UNITY OF OPPOSITES

. . . We encounter the anima historically above all in the divine syzygies, the male-female pairs of deities. These reach down, on the one side, into the obscurities of primitive mythology, and up, on the other, into the philosophical speculations of Gnosticism and of classical Chinese philosophy, where the cosmogonic pair of concepts are designated *yang* (masculine) and *yin* (feminine). We can safely assert that these syzygies are as universal as the existence of man and woman. From this fact we may reasonably conclude that man's imagination is bound by this motif, so that he was largely compelled to project it again and again, at all times and in all places.[10]

We experience the Shadow as that which is completely different from ourself, totally "other." If we

---

[10]Carl Jung, *Collected Works*, Vol. 9, I, 120.

acknowledge the Shadow, eventually we come to discover that it is, in fact, a necessary part of the personality. We then come to what I have characterized as the Shadow stage of the Anima/Animus. Once more, our initial experience is of something totally different from what we consider ourselves to be. We then discover that those traits that we previously considered as belonging exclusively to the opposite sex, belong to us as well. In both cases, if we look closely enough, we see ourselves peering back, as if in a mirror.

When we arrive at the archetypal Anima/Animus, once again we experience something opposite to ourselves. But this time, as we dig deeper, we don't see ourselves looking back; instead it is our complement, that which we need to make us whole. Think of all the pairs of opposites we deal with day in and day out—hot/cold, active/passive, hard/soft, thinking/feeling, sensation/intuition, aggressive/receptive, etc. Each is defined by its opposite: without hot, there isn't any such thing as cold; without cold, what would hot mean? When we think of any of these paired qualities, we always have their opposite in mind, consciously or unconsciously.

Separating these pairs into opposing groups, then referring to one group of traits as feminine and the other as masculine, is at best a crude approximation to the reality we all experience. Like all other pairs of opposites, masculine and feminine are inseparable concepts, each of which in large part defines its opposite. The I Ching uses the terms Yin and Yang to present this concept of paired opposites, and though Yin is more often associated with the feminine, and Yang with the masculine, in the words of Cole Porter, "it ain't necessarily so."

Significantly the pairing of Yin and Yang is presented as a circle with a wavy line cutting it in half. One side is light, one dark. But if we look more closely, we can see a tiny dark wavy half-circle within the light side, a tiny light

Figure 15. Anima within the animus. Our psyche is comprised of layer upon layer. In dealing with the anima or animus, we deal with a whole chain of complex relationships between pairs of opposites, such as the masculine and the feminine. (Reprinted from *1001 Spot Illustrations of the Lively Twenties*.)

half-circle within the dark side. And within each of those, we would find the same process repeated, ad infinitum. This symbolizes the unity that lies within opposition that is central to understanding the Oriental concept of Yin and Yang (and equally the Anima/Animus).

> Although man and woman unite they neverthe-less represent irreconcilable opposites. . . . This primordial pair of opposites symbolizes every con-ceivable pair of opposites that may occur: hot and cold, light and dark, north and south, dry and damp, good and bad, conscious and uncon-scious.[11]

If men and women have sharply defined roles within a culture, so, too, will they have a sharply defined Anima or Animus in the unconscious, which complements that one-sidedness, in much the same way as the Shadow comple-ments a too one-sided self-definition. But if we look closer, we will find that the Anima itself contains masculine traits that complement it in turn. Within that masculine are fur-ther feminine traits to complement the masculine, and so forth. If we could follow the chain from consciousness,

---

[11]Carl Jung, *The Collected Works*, Vol. 12: *Psychology and Alchemy*, copy-right 1953, © 1968 (Princeton: Princeton University Press), 192.

deeper and deeper into the unconscious, we would find little or no masculine psychological experience not available to women, or feminine experience not available to men.

In other words, the Anima and Animus are not defined so much by particular traits, set for all time, as they are by the complementary nature of the relationship between male and female. We experience both the physical world and the psyche through the inner lens of that complementary relationship. As that relationship changes, so does our inner lens; i.e., the Anima/Animus evolves.

Therefore, perhaps we can get some further understanding of the archetype of the Anima/Animus by examining the evolution, over time, of relationships between men and women. Let's begin with the most recent major shift in that relationship—the birth of romantic love.

CHIVALRY AND THE GRAIL LEGEND

The concept of romantic love is quite modern: it first appeared in the 12th century under the guise of chivalry. Central to chivalry was a strange new variation on the relationship between men and women—courtly love. Before chivalry, the world had not yet developed an explicit concept of "pure" love between man and woman, uncontaminated by sexuality. With the advent of chivalry, men suddenly developed an ideal view of women, which was distinctly separate from mere lust.

In this idealized picture, the woman was regarded by the male as pure and undefiled, the male by the female as brave and equally pure. They viewed their relationship as beyond "mere" sexuality. What made this idea so incredible was that the woman was already married to another man and, therefore, obviously sexually active (so hardly

Figure 16. The appearance of courtly love in Europe in the 12th century was the first sign of a major transition beginning in the psyche. (Reprinted from *Pictorial Archive of Decorative Renaissance Woodcuts*.)

"undefiled"). Yet this fact was totally ignored by the man, a sure sign that an archetypal projection was taking place. Correspondingly, the woman projected a new vision of her lover as a virtuous knight who would overcome any obstacle ("slay any dragon") in order to protect her honor. Again this new concept was completely asexual; the knight even took vows of chastity (though this was more honored in the promise than in the practice).

The epitome of such a knight was Parsifal in his search for the Grail. The Grail legend appeared contemporaneously with chivalry and seems to have no archetypal precedent. In summary, the legend began with an aged king, who had been wounded in the thigh. The king can be seen as representing an outmoded masculine approach to life. The wound to the thigh is symbolic of a wound to his instinctual/sexual nature. With the king lying deathly ill, the affairs of his kingdom come to a halt. That is, there can be no further growth until some solution is found to this problem. The only thing that can cure the king is the Grail cup: the cup which Jesus used at the Last Supper to change wine into blood. The Grail symbolizes the missing feminine element which the aged king lacks in his life.

Only a knight pure in thought and deed can find the Grail. That is, only a man who can relate to the feminine separate from his sexual desires can find the Grail. Of course, if there is such a man, he already *has* found the Grail; that is, he has already found the missing feminine element inside himself. In which case, there would be no need for a quest. Therefore, the real purpose of the quest is to present the knight with a series of trials which gradually awaken him to the feminine part of his true nature. Unfortunately, in none of the many versions of the Grail legend is the knight totally successful—the reason being that there was, then, no way for the masculine to fully relate to the feminine except through sexuality. A new archetypal relationship was trying to emerge, but it was premature.

The story is about the male's search for the missing feminine element, not the female's search for the missing masculine, though both are necessary. This is because the world at large has always been under the control of men, with the feminine viewpoint restricted to the subsidiary role of the home. This made it highly unlikely that the male could find the missing feminine until women had an equal say in the world.

ANIMA/ANIMUS IN RELATIONSHIPS

Gradually, over the next eight hundred years, there was some integration of this new aspect of the Anima/Animus, as evidenced by the advance in the state of women. Where once marriage was an economic relationship, now in the so-called developed nations, it is taken for granted that love is the chief reason for marriage. This is so widely accepted that, when love ends, marriage is now most often dissolved through divorce. This is a very, very recent attitude and can be seen as an unprecedented experiment in the evolution of the Anima/Animus. Under this new set of rules, men and women have been forced to find mates who closely match their inner personification of the ideal woman or man. The high divorce rates are an indication that, most of the time, this attempt has not been successful.

In our discussion of the Shadow, we have already seen how initial projections are vague and inchoate, far from a person's particular Shadow. Similarly, initial Anima/Animus projections are crude and have little to do with the unique contra-sexual identity we seek.

There is a built-in push to integrate the Shadow, which doesn't necessarily occur with the Anima/Animus. When we ignore Shadow qualities long enough, they are projected outward. And because they are normally connected with negative feelings, this leads to conflicts in the outer world. Since most of us want to avoid conflict, we are forced to come to some degree of recognition of our Shadow. Of course, this is hardly universal. The Cold War of Shadow projections between the United States and

Russia lasted over forty years. We have all seen people who grow more, not less, bigoted across time. But most people gradually develop some increase in tolerance, which leads to a development of their own personality.

The Anima/Animus projection is more complex. As with Shadow projections, when the need for a connection to one's contra-sexual qualities becomes strong enough, the Anima or Animus is projected out onto a person of the opposite sex. But in this case, it is an attraction coupled with desirable qualities which is projected, rather than a repulsion coupled with negative feelings. In other words, we fall in love. It is a wonderfully pleasant feeling to fall in love. Even the bitter-sweet pangs of longing for an unrequited love is preferable to the blah state of mind in which most of life goes past.

Unfortunately, when we see the real person emerge from behind the projection, it is far easier to break up with that person and wait to "fall in love" again than it is to work our way toward a real relationship.

On the other hand, because we are attracted to the lover, and dote on every quality (even though we don't realize that these qualities are largely our own, and don't belong to the lover), we come to observe and relate to parts of ourself we wouldn't otherwise notice. A woman's receptivity brings out a man's strength, and vice versa. Both men and women learn how wonderfully freeing it is to return to the playfulness of childhood once more with a lover. Both learn how relaxing it is to be able to release control, if only for the moment of sexual release. Each learns to respect the body, because the lover desires it so much.

If a relationship develops, deeper aspects are revealed. A woman discovers the insecurities that lie beneath masculine bravado and loves the man more dearly. The man finds out that a seemingly "weak" woman is frequently the stronger of the two when a real

Figure 17.   Animus in the Driver's Seat. When we fall into moods and opinions, it is wise to remember that it is often because the anima or animus is in the driver's seat. (Reprinted from *Humorous Victorian Spot Illustrations*.)

crisis affects their lives. A woman notices just how fragile the structure of a man's seemingly impenetrable "rational" approach to reality can be.

Women beat in frustration against the wall of a man's emotional indifference. Men beat in frustration against the wall of a woman's emotional withdrawal. Both have to learn how to contain that frustration. Women discover that a man can't contain his anger without releasing it in some physical action (unfortunately far too often beating the woman). In contrast, men discover just how intensely a woman's anger can burn without any physical release. These discoveries (and many others) are usually unique to the relationship between men and women. Unless one perseveres in a relationship, these discoveries about one another are never made, and the man and the woman will be the poorer for never encountering them.

Previously, I mentioned George Vallant's insight that the surest prediction of mental health was the ability to sustain a long-term relationship: "It's not that divorce is unhealthy or bad, but that loving people for long periods of time is good." Two things happen when we love someone for a long time:

1) we get to know them better; and

2) we get to know ourselves better.

That's why I said that this modern development of love between the sexes has been an unprecedented experiment. For thousands of years, the relationship between men and women remained relatively unchanged. Then suddenly something new came into the world—romantic love! And everything was changed forever.

THE FEMININE WORLD TO COME

. . . The solemn proclamation of the *Assumptio Mariae* [author's note: the Assumption of Mary, mother of Jesus] which we have experienced in our own day is an example of the way symbols develop through the ages. The impelling motive behind it did not come from the ecclesiastical authorities, who had given clear proof of their hesitation by postponing the declaration for nearly a hundred years, but from the Catholic masses, who have insisted more and more vehemently on this development. This insistence is, at bottom, the urge of the archetype to realize itself.[12]

Jung thought he heard the first sounds of something momentous when the Catholic Church formally proclaimed the Assumption of Mary, the mother of Jesus, in 1950. (In Catholic theology, the Assumption of Mary is the doctrine that after her death, Mary, like Jesus, was taken bodily into heaven. This gives her a unique status – almost godlike – since it is Catholic doctrine that body and soul separate at death, to be reunited again only at the time of the Last Judgment.) Jung felt that Mary provided the missing fourth element – a feminine element – which completed the trinity of God the Father, Son, and Holy Ghost, and made it into a quaternity, which Jung felt represented wholeness. (We will have much more to say about quaternities and mandalas, inner symbols of wholeness, in the next chapter on the Self.)

By 1950, Jung had already seen the collapse of many of the masculine values which had ruled the world for so long. We, who are now living in the late days of the 20th century, have seen virtually all those structures crumble around us – political, economic, scientific, artistic, cultural, religious, etc. All the "rational" structures which have developed and sustained us over so many centuries have suddenly become inadequate to deal with the newly revealed complexity of the world.

In our frustration with the old ways, we've turned toward previously unnoticed cultural influences: Eastern philosophy and mysticism, Native American values and ceremonies are two examples. Another has been the rise of the Civil Rights movement. No longer willing to be swallowed up in the melting pot, minorities have begun to insist on retaining their separate identities. But perhaps

---

[12]Carl Jung, *Collected Works*, Vol. 9, II, 142.

the most important of all these new elements of change came when the "majority minority" took the stage—the women's movement.

Currently, we live in an inchoate period when seemingly all we know is that we don't know much of anything. Traditional values no longer work, but we don't yet know what to substitute for those outmoded convictions. Nowhere is this more clearly symbolized than in the changing relationship between men and women. It is clear to me (and to many others) that women's values are in the first inchoate stages of becoming the ruling values. Though men (and women who are more comfortable with masculine rule) are fighting this change tooth-and-nail, men's values and institutions are gradually retreating, like the slow withdrawal of an ice age.

We see reminders of the masculine view of the world everywhere around us. If the feminine viewpoint is represented at all, it is only seen through the lens of the masculine Anima, and a crude, undeveloped Anima at that. However, even that appearance (for example, in the open acknowledgment of pornography) is a sign that the feminine is coming forth. (Not that women encourage pornography; rather that the feminine in men is emerging whether or not the men want it to emerge.) We aren't likely to see the full complexity of feminine values until women are in positions of power and prestige and, unfortunately, that hasn't happened yet.

Nonetheless, the Anima is being projected onto the world, and both men and women are noticing that the fit between the feminine as represented by the Anima, and the feminine as represented by real women, is clearly not very good. Just as in a mutual Anima/Animus projection between an individual man and woman, this either leads to a deepening of the relationship (with concomitant growth for both), or the relationship breaks off, until the next projection takes place. So far, in the broader projection of the Anima out onto the world, we've got a lot more of the latter than the former, but some men and women are "deepening the relationship" between masculine and feminine. It will inevitably continue.

Men are in charge everywhere, and masculine values predominate. Therefore, for once it is men who will have to open themselves and accept the seed of the new, bear it inside themselves, carry it patiently to term, and suffer the pains of the labor necessary to give birth—in this case, to give birth to the new feminine world. In contrast, women are in an equally uncharacteristic position. They have planted the seed, and are now champing at the bit, eager for the birth to take place.

Since it is the missing feminine that will come to dominate the future world, it is incumbent on men to come to terms with the Anima. Women also need to find reconciliation with the Animus inside them. Otherwise, they are likely to be satisfied with a simple change of command, with masculine values still predominating, even though expressed by women. The more fully women understand both the strengths and weaknesses of the masculine world-view, the more able they will be to successfully lead the new world to come.

CHAPTER 7

THE SELF

The Self can be the dreamer's deepest personality, the process of development, and the goal of the process, all wrapped up in one entity. Equally the Self transcends all limits of personal morality, yet its ethics possess a rightness at some deep level that cannot be denied.

—R. Robertson

In chapter 5, we defined the Self in brief as an inner template for the person we are intended to become. As such, it is a goal always ahead, never quite reached. But it is much more than that. The Self is the "god within," the closest psychological approximation to the godhead, capable of provoking the wonder and awe we usually associate with encounters with divinity. (We already alluded to this numinous quality of the collective unconscious in chapter 4 during our discussion of the inferior function.) Finally, the Self is also the "transcendent function" which establishes wholeness and order within the psyche.

The Self clothes itself in many personalized forms—stretching all the way from animal to human to godlike.

But it can also pick impersonal forms—a lake, a mountain, a rose, a tree. It may even appear in abstract geometric forms called *mandalas*, which we will discuss later in this chapter. Clearly, the Self—as both the source of the individuation process and its ultimate goal—is beyond rigid definition. Let's begin by discussing its numinous aspect as "the god within."

THE GOD WITHIN US

[The integration of the Anima/Animus] leads us, by a natural route, back to . . . "something" [that] is strange to us and yet so near, wholly ourselves and yet unknowable, a virtual centre of so mysterious a constitution that it can claim anything— kinship with beasts and gods, with crystals and with stars—without moving us to wonder, without even exciting our disapprobation. This "something" claims all that and more, and having nothing in our hands that could fairly be opposed to these claims, it is surely wiser to listen to this voice. . . . I have called this centre the *self*. . . . It might equally well be called the "God within us."[1]

Jung was neither asserting nor denying the existence of a literal God. He was describing a psychological reality, not a metaphysical reality. He was merely presenting something he had encountered time after time in his work with his patients, in his own life, and in his studies of mythology; i.e., at a certain depth in the psyche, numinous forces are awakened which we experience as godlike.

Jung felt it was wrong to deny psychological experience just because it didn't fit conveniently into a belief

---

[1]Carl Jung, *Collected Works*, Vol. 7, 398–399.

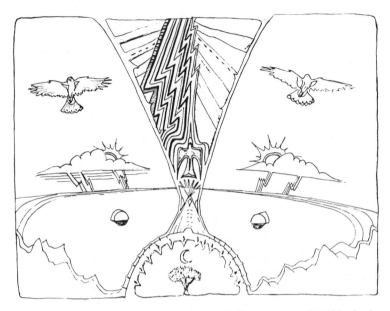

Figure 18.   Emerging Self. We can only find our essential Self by look-ing deep within. When the Self emerges from the unconscious, it is often accompanied by "lightning and thunder," which breaks apart the symmetry of our previous consciousness. (Drawing by patient, 1981.)

system. His openness to unusual phenomena never fal-tered throughout his life. You will recall from chapter 1 that, while in college, Jung was amazed at the resistance of his classmates, who refused to even consider the possibil-ity that paranormal events could occur. Though they dis-missed such events with contempt, to Jung their uneasi-ness seemed at odds with their alleged surety. Jung believed that if ordinary people experienced phenomena like ghosts, for example, then ghosts must correspond to something significant in the psyche, regardless of the physical existence or non-existence of ghosts.

Similarly, Jung could not accept Freud's insistence that at all costs, he must preserve psychoanalysis against the "black mud of occultism." For Jung, all human experience was worthy of description, and any model of reality worthy of the name had to include all human experience, not merely those experiences which fit a particular theory.

Because he presented the Self as a psychological reality which paralleled the concept of God, Jung was criticized by the religious as well as by the materialists. The religious accused Jung of trying to reduce God to a psychological function, while the materialists accused him of trying to substitute metaphysics for science. It is hard to walk the razor's edge between those two camps, but Jung was willing to attempt no less.

Though he always firmly denied that his model had any metaphysical reality, he did argue that if a God existed, the only way God could be experienced would be through some such psychological function as the Self. In other words, if we don't already have within ourselves some experience which corresponds to divinity, we couldn't apprehend divinity at all. Regardless of whether or not a literal God exists, the fact that we innately possess an archetype of the numinous indicates that it is a necessary component of psychological wholeness.[2]

In presenting his three-stage model of the individuation process, Jung was trying to describe observable facts. In portraying each stage in terms of a personalized figure—1) the Shadow, 2) the Anima/Animus, and 3) the Self—he was presenting "an abbreviated description or definition of these facts."[3] This personalization wasn't Jung's invention: he observed it in his own dreams and

---

[2]Carl Jung, *Collected Works*, Vol. 7, 402.
[3]Carl Jung, *Collected Works*, Vol. 9, II, 63.

the dreams of his patients. The psyche itself chose to personalize.[4]

It is one thing to dismiss the literal reality of so-called primitive religious experience, it is quite another to attempt to dismiss the psychological reality of that experience. Anyone who encounters the Self invariably feels that numinous quality that we rightly associate with divinity. One can no more communicate the experience of the Self to someone who has never had such an experience, than one can describe the experience of love to someone who has never been in love.

The Self is not limited by our expectations of morality, our concerns are not necessarily its concerns. This amoral, inhuman aspect of the Self is far too frequently overlooked by people who talk blithely about finding the Higher Self, or their Guardian Angel. Real encounters with the Self can be terrifying and incomprehensible.

This was an issue that occupied Jung throughout his life. He dealt with it most fully in a very late essay,

---

[4]Carl Jung, *Collected Works*, Vol. 13, 61. Interested readers should also know that Jung always went out of his way to point out not only the strengths, but the limitations of this model, and to look for other models. Jung's second great model of the psyche came about through his study of alchemy. He discovered that, because the early alchemists were still psychologically naive, they projected their unconscious processes out into their alchemical experiments. Since they were striving after the unattainable (the Philosopher's Stone which would cure all sickness, turn lead into gold, and bestow immortality upon the alchemist), they could not possibly reach their final goal—just as it is impossible to ever fully integrate the unconscious into consciousness. Accordingly, their carefully described experimental accounts can be interpreted psychologically as a wonderfully complete model of the process of psychological development. Unfortunately, the details of his alchemical model lie beyond the scope of this book.

"Answer to Job."[5] Jung examined Job's behavior toward God and God's behavior toward Job, and found Job came out the winner. God was presented as a petulant and irrational tyrant, while Job was both loyal and thoughtful. Jung felt that the story of Job marked a turning point in consciousness when God was forced to acknowledge Job as his moral superior. God was for the first time forced to consider the possibility of a true relationship with mankind—which would eventually lead to the appearance of Jesus, who combined God and man in a single being.

As might be expected, this was a highly controversial stance which won Jung many enemies. Jung was never able to get his critics to understand that he was talking about a psychological reality, not a metaphysical reality. To Jung, the Bible was a record of the evolution of humanity's conception of the divine. When he talked of the God of the Bible, Jung meant the Self, "the god within." Job represented the state of conscious development of humanity at a unique point in time: from that point on, conscious and unconscious were forced to find a point of rapprochement.

This struggle still goes on within our individual psyches, and is reflected in our dreams. Each of us reaches a point in life when it is no longer enough to live life unconsciously. In our attempts to become conscious, we are forced on a long journey that inevitably brings us—like Job—to a confrontation with the Self. There we are forced to acknowledge its inhuman aspect, which is presented in the story of Job when God tells Job that he created the leviathan and the behemoth. That moment of awakening is always a heroic struggle, and few possess the courage of Job when exposed to the terrifying energy of the Self. Job

---

[5]Carl Jung, *The Collected Works*, Vol. 11: *Psychology and Religion: West and East*, copyright © 1958, 1969 (Princeton: Princeton University Press), 553–758.

reveals the proper response to such inhuman power: bow your head and acknowledge the superior strength—but don't give up your values! Jung had a similar image in an important dream: kneel, bow your head, but don't quite let your forehead touch the ground.

The experience of the "god within" can take many different forms, from a literal belief that one has encountered Jesus or Buddha, to the equally religious fervor characteristic of social reformers, or even scientists. Jung often pointed out that the zeal of materialist scientists to discover the ultimate secrets of the universe is essentially an unacknowledged religious belief.

An example would be the subatomic physicists of today, who are convinced that they are about to put together a comprehensive "grand unification theory" which will explain everything in the universe once and for all. Obviously there is no such final explanation. Science is based on the provisional nature of all its theories; after all, scientific "laws" are only models that proved effective in describing and predicting natural behavior. Eventually all scientific laws are either overturned or subsumed within more encompassing models.

It is wise to be aware of the psychological reality of the Self, and that an archetype is at work. The absolute surety of our inner experience may have little or nothing to do with its outer truth. (This is a concept that fundamentalists of all faiths should keep in mind more often.)

MANDALAS

Although "wholeness" seems at first sight to be nothing but an abstract idea (like anima or animus), it is nevertheless empirical in so far as it is anticipated by the psyche in the form of spontane-

ous or autonomous symbols. These are the quaternity or mandala symbols.[6]

The Self presents itself to consciousness in a dizzying
variety of forms. This is a simple consequence of the fact
that the Self is further away from consciousness than
either the Shadow or the Anima/Animus. All archetypes
are experienced as true symbols: a symbol can't be
reduced to a single definition or a simple sign; a symbol is
open to many interpretations. But as we progress deeper
into the collective unconscious, an archetype is forced to
express itself in an ever wider variety of forms when presented to consciousness, in order to gets its message
across. And since the Self is the supreme archetype, it is
the most difficult to capture or understand.

In our progressive model of individuation, where the
Shadow represents the despised "other," and the Anima/
Animus represents relationship, the Self most often repre-
sents wholeness. In its most extreme abstract form, the
Self takes the form of geometric figures called *mandalas*.

Mandala is a Sanskrit word meaning circle, which has
been generalized further to describe a type of Oriental
religious art structured around circles contained within
squares (or sometimes other regular polygons), or vice
versa. Many of the religious sand paintings of the Navajo
Indians in America have a similar structure, as do numerous other religious symbols throughout the world. In Oriental traditions, the mandala is usually a subject for meditation and contemplation, with the intent of leading the
meditator progressively deeper into an inner unity with
the godhead (in whatever form, abstract or personified,
the godhead takes in those various cultures).

Jung was fascinated by the fact that mandalas showed
up quite frequently in the dreams of his patients, nearly

---

[6]Carl Jung, *Collected Works*, Vol. 9, II, 59.

Figure 19. Symmetric figures called mandalas often appear in dreams or spontaneous drawings at times when order is being restored in the psyche. (Mandalas produced over a two-week period in 1980.)

always at a time when they were attempting to restore inner wholeness. In Jung's estimation, the circle was a representation of the ultimate wholeness only possible to the Self; the square was sort of an inferior circle, and represented the limited wholeness possible to individual ego consciousness. Mandalas, as a combination of circle and square, reflected an attempt by the psyche to "square the circle" and bring the limited wholeness possible to the individual into synchrony with the Self.

Just imagine the four-sided square doubling to become a regular eight-sided octagon, then a regular sixteen-sided figure, etc. Eventually, it would be impossible for the human eye to detect the difference between the many-sided figure and a circle. But a high-enough powered microscope would still reveal that it wasn't a circle.

Just as we could trace the progression of a square becoming more and more like a circle, as the number of its sides doubles, it is possible to follow the progression of consciousness toward the Self, by observing the evolution of such symbols of wholeness in dreams. This may sound incredible; however, Jung in fact did trace such a progression of dreams—not once, but twice![7]

More recently, art therapist Rhoda Kellog discovered that the drawings of preschool children progress from initial scribbles, to crosses, then to crosses within circles, which is a basic mandala form. Their first attempts to draw the full human figure almost invariably are not the stick figures we might expect, but circles.[8]

It is important to understand what wholeness means in the psyche. Most of us are accustomed to linear goals:

---

[7]Carl Jung, "A Study in the Process of Individuation," *Collected Works*, Vol. 9, I, 525–626; and "Individual Dream Symbolism in Relation to Alchemy," *Collected Works*, Vol. 12, 44–331.

[8]See Edward Edinger, *Ego and Archetype* (Baltimore, MD: Penguin Books, 1972), p. 8, for details and reproductions of the children's drawings.

we seek perfection, not wholeness or completeness. If we get a score of 80 on a paper, we try to get an 85 the next time, then 90, 95, 100. When we reach 100 and can go no higher, we set a new goal. Our moral goals are essentially the same: deny the dark and seek the light, climb ever higher toward perfection, etc. But, as we found in studying the Shadow, light isn't enough; a well-rounded personality needs the darkness as well.

> . . . otherwise one will never attain that median degree of modesty which is essential for the maintenance of a balanced state. *It is not a question, as one might think, of relaxing morality itself but of making a moral effort in a different direction.*[9]

"A moral effort in a different direction"—a strange concept for those of us raised on American verities, where morality is supposedly simple and straightforward, and dictated by an inner guide—our conscience. Unfortunately, that supposed conscience is nothing more than an internalization of parents and all other voices of authority we have heard throughout our lives. The voice of the Self is something quite different; it has an authority that transcends those personal parental voices. And its counsel is not for perfection, but for wholeness.

THE TRANSCENDENT FUNCTION

In tracing the path of individuation, we started with Jung's discovery that there is no single appropriate developmental path for all people, because people are different psychological types. For example, an appropriate path for an introverted feeler is far different from the path appropriate

---

[9]Carl Jung, *Collected Works*, Vol. 9, II, 47. Italics added.

for an extraverted thinker. They are so different in the way they approach reality that it would be criminal to force either to be like the other.

We found that, as life progresses, and people become too fixed in their personal types, the Shadow appears. It is fascinating to note that the Shadow doesn't take a single form; the various psychological types have Shadows with very different personality characteristics, though we all would initially perceive the Shadow as repulsive and frightening. This tailoring of the Shadow to fit our individual needs is an indication that a "transcendent function" exists which encompasses both our conscious personality and the Shadow.

Think about how strange this really is. How is it that at every stage of our development, the unconscious is able to appropriately compensate for our conscious extremes? This seems to indicate that there must be some inner definition of what our ideal self should be at each point in our development. How else can we account for the fact that when we are near that ideal, our dreams closely reflect our outer reality, and when we stray too far from that ideal, our dreams are at wide variance with our outer experience?

You will remember from chapter 2 Konrad Lorenz' discovery of the imprinting process in animals. In brief, inborn behaviors (which Jung called archetypes and I have also called cognitive invariants) were triggered by appropriate outer stimuli at key times in the animal's development. Though I used the example of a baby goose imprinting the Mother Archetype onto Lorenz, there are a wide variety of cognitive invariants which are imprinted during an animal's development.

Famed biologist and child psychologist Jean Piaget carefully recorded a similar process in the development of human children. Various skills are triggered at just the appropriate time in a child's development. Before that time, it is useless to try and force the child into a behavior he or she is not ready for, such as toilet-training too early. One day, a child will be unable to grasp a concept, and then seemingly overnight, he or she will have no further trouble with that concept.

Jung's study of the individuation process, as mirrored in our dreams, reveals that this is an exact process; at every moment in our development, our psyche contains a portrait of what we, at our best, can be. This ideal self is the center around which both our conscious ego and our unconscious Shadow revolve in perfect balance. When our conscious personality moves too far from that ideal, a compensating Shadow figure forms in the unconscious. When our conscious personality comes closer to that ideal, so does the Shadow; it becomes less evil and despised, more like our conscious personality. This transcendent function literally transcends both conscious and unconscious.

> There is nothing mysterious or metaphysical about the term "transcendent function." It means a psychological function comparable in its way to a mathematical function of the same name, which is a function of real and imaginary numbers. The psychological "transcendent function" arises from the union of conscious and unconscious contents.[10]

I hope readers will bear with me in a brief discussion of the mathematical history of transcendent functions. I promise it won't be too painful and that it will shed some light on the Self. The transcendent functions which Jung refers to in mathematics are more often called "complex numbers." In solving many equations, mathematicians found that the square root of (– 1) appeared as part of the

[10]Carl Jung, *Collected Works*, Vol. 8, 131.

answer. At first, these results were dismissed out of hand, since how could any number have a negative square root?[11]

However, it was so useful to pretend that such numbers could exist that mathematicians continued to use them. To indicate that they didn't really believe these numbers existed, they termed them imaginary, and used the shorthand sign "i" to indicate such numbers. They were then able to make up "complex numbers" (or "transcendent functions" as Jung termed them) using combinations of "real" numbers and "imaginary" numbers (e.g., [3 – 5i]; [– 6 + 2i], etc.).

Subsequently, early in the 19th century, one of the greatest mathematicians of all time, Karl Friedrich Gauss, came up with a geometric interpretation which made imaginary numbers acceptable. Imagine two lines at right angles to one another. Anything lying on the horizontal line to the right of where they meet is a positive number (+ 1, + 2, + 3, . . .), anything to the left is a negative number (– 1, – 2, – 3, . . .). Where the two lines meet is called the "origin" and has the value 0. Anything on the vertical line above the origin is a positive imaginary number (+ i, + 2i, + 3i, . . .), anything below the origin is a negative imaginary number (– i, – 2i, – 3i, . . .).

Any point on the plane defined by the two lines can be located in terms of how far it is to the right or left, and how far up or down. For example, the point 2 unit lengths to the right of the origin and 2 above the origin, can be uniquely defined by the coordinate (2, 2). Similarly, (3, – 6) would be a spot three units to the right of the origin and 6 below. (3, – 6) stands not only for that partic-

---

[11]The square root of a number is the number, which when multiplied by itself, gives the original number. For example, either + 2 or – 2 is the square root of + 4, since (+ 2) times (+ 2) equals + 4, and (– 2) times (– 2) equals + 4.

ular point on the plane, but also for the mathematical expression (+ 3 – 6i). Suddenly mathematical problems which involved complex numbers could be simply described by drawing various geometric figures on the plane.

If this sounds exotic, it's the same system that we use to give street addresses in a large town, such as "524 East 87th Street." Streets are laid out at right angles to each other, and numbered in each direction. The location of any house can be uniquely described by two numbers—the numbered street name (East 87th Street) and the street address (524).[12]

All right, enough mathematics. Let's just look at that mathematical history and see if it sheds light on Jung's psychological concept of the transcendent function. Initially, when imaginary numbers showed up as the solution for equations, mathematicians ignored them as impossible. Gradually, they began to use them and even developed a symbol system for their use, but they still condemned them as "imaginary." Still they were willing to combine so-called "real numbers" and "imaginary numbers" into "complex numbers" (or "transcendent functions" as Jung described them). Finally, Gauss realized that mathematicians were restricting themselves unnecessarily by limiting their frame of reference to the line of positive and negative numbers. He extended the field of discussion to the whole plane, and complex numbers became simple descriptions of locations on the plane.

Compare this to the concept of the collective unconscious. Initially psychologists preferred to ignore such a possibility. As collective archetypes kept cropping up in

---

[12]I am indebted to Jungian analyst J. Marvin Spiegelman for the insight that complex numbers are a metaphor for the relationship between the ego and the Self.

dreams, many psychologists began using interpretations which depended on knowledge of archetypal histories such as mythology. But they still insisted that they were just discussing metaphors. If something like the Self should seem to exist which was a combination of conscious (hence real) and unconscious (hence imaginary), it could only be a metaphor. Jung argued that it was time to acknowledge the reality of such a transcendent function. In order to do so, we need to extend our frame of reference from the linear frame of consciousness to the plane which includes both consciousness and the unconscious.

Now we can move to discuss some of the practical considerations in dealing with the Self.

THE SELF IN DREAMS

We have discussed how the mandala images occur in dreams at a time when the psyche is trying to restore wholeness. Many of these depict an attempt to "square the circle." Similarly, dreams that exhibit combinations of threes and fours also appear at such times. As we mentioned earlier, Jung saw the Christian Trinity as an incomplete quaternity, because a feminine element was missing. In a cycle of dreams, dreams with threes occur when some resolution for a problem is just starting to emerge. When the issue has progressed far enough that the psyche is ready for healing, those threes give way to fours.

Mandalas sometimes appear in a dream directly as abstract geometric figures, like a square within a circle, a triangle within a square (or more exotic variations on these themes). More frequently, however, the mandala image will be found in the structure of the dream's action. For example, a friend reported a dream in which he was playing a card game that used three decks of cards. He had eight 3s in his hand. (When 4 progresses to 8, to 16, to 32, etc., it is an indication that the issue has progressed as well; i.e., an 8 is sort of a super 4 in dreams.)

The image of squaring the circle may take the form of a dream where a group of people move in a circle inside a square room. In early dreams, the room is often an exaggerated rectangle that slowly evolves into a square in later dreams. The people will move around the room in a clockwise direction (to the right, to the side of consciousness) when an issue is emerging into consciousness, counterclockwise (to the left, the side of the unconscious) when it is retreating from conscious awareness into the unconscious.

When wholeness is restored in the psyche, some dramatic example of a mandala often appears in a dream: for example, a circular island, with a square city in the middle. In the middle of the city, further series of circular shapes and square shapes appear, culminating in a castle or a church, etc. Jung, himself, had such a dream at a critical point in his own self-development, and this dream led him to his understanding of the Self.

> . . . It goes without saying that the self also has its theriomorphic symbolism. The commonest of these images in modern dreams are, in my experience, the elephant, horse, bull, bear, white and black birds, fishes, and snakes. Occasionally one comes across tortoises, snails, spiders and beetles. The principal plant symbols are the flower and the tree. Of the inorganic products, the commonest are the mountain and lake.[13]

Theriomorphic dreams, in which the Self is clothed in the form of an animal, are often numinous dreams that leave the dreamer in awe upon awakening. This numinous feeling far exceeds the overt content of the dream,

---

[13]Carl Jung, *Collected Works*, Vol. 9, II, 356.

Figure 20. Animal Self Behind Bars. Because we often experience the Self as inhuman and terrifying, it is frequently represented in dreams by a powerful animal, like a lion or a bear. Because of our fear, we must try to keep that powerful instinctual side of us behind bars, hidden from consciousness, but it always emerges eventually. (From *Don Quichotte de le Manche*. Reprinted from *Dore's Spot Illustrations*.)

and is an indication of the powerful archetypal force of the symbol. These dreams often mark the earliest appearance of the Self, similar to the initial appearance of the Shadow as an inhuman creature. However, the dream reaction to the animals that represent the Self is wonder (or wonder mixed with fear), rather than the revulsion we feel toward the inhuman Shadow.

When an animal exhibits a sense of detachment, as if the world it inhabits has little or no connection with humanity, it is a clue that the animal represents the Self. Reptiles best typify this cold-blooded quality. In our earlier discussion of Paul MacLean's triune model of the brain, we learned that we contain a reptile brain that experiences reality much as reptiles experienced reality a quarter of a billion years ago. That's a very long time ago, yet even by that time, the evolution of life had already progressed for two to three billion years. The Self reflects not just the short period of human history (which we tend to confuse with all history), but those two to three billion years as well.

Reptiles—especially snakes—often appear in dreams at a time when a new life cycle is beginning. They are a reminder of the Self's twin aspects: instinctive power and wisdom. A wise first approximation to the Self is to see it as the total mind/body, especially if we can capitalize Body to indicate something more than a machine. The self-regulation of the psyche is much more akin to the self-regulation of the body than it is to some independent agent sitting apart from us, watching over our every deed.

But as soon as we begin to think that we can limit the psyche to some super-hormonal reaction, it will suddenly surprise us with the depth of its knowledge. Jung often remarked that it can be wiser to treat the Self less as instinct and more like a God. Again, Jung wasn't making a metaphysical judgment when he said this; he had observed that when the unconscious is approached with reverence, life goes on more swimmingly.

Animals, as images of the Self, frequently preside over transformation in dreams. Kafka's famous story, "Metamorphosis," in which the protagonist wakes to find himself transformed into a beetle, is an example of a frequent dream image of transformation. When we have gone through a major life change, especially without realizing we have done so, the world becomes so very strange, that the only satisfactory self-image is grotesque and inhuman—like Kafka's beetle.

The mountain, the ocean, and the tree are frequent images of the Self. But the Self can also appear in simpler, less exalted forms, such as a flower (often a rose), a tranquil lake, a winding path. Jung studied the image of the tree in the dreams and paintings of his patients, as well as in mythology, and published his results in an extended essay called "The Philosophical Tree."

> . . . If a mandala may be described as symbol of the self seen in cross section, then the tree would represent a profile view of it: the self depicted as a process of growth.[14]

A tree is an exceptionally fine image of the Self as a "process of growth." The trunk of the tree lives and grows in the world as we know it (as do we all). From that fixed point, it spreads forth in the twin directions of earth and sky. The roots grow deep into the ground, which signifies the instinctual "ground" of all life. (Cut off from our instincts, we perish just as surely as a tree without its roots.) But the tree needs equally to grow branches and leaves that reach out into the sky to absorb the sun's energy. This is a perfect picture of the human need for

---

[14]Carl Jung, *Collected Works*, Vol. 13, 304–482.

spiritual values; without a deep and abiding connection to something bigger than human, we all wither and die.

A tree is such a good metaphor that it often appears in dreams at key moments in our development. For example, one patient dreamed he was in a park filled with trees. When he looked closer, he saw that the roots of the trees not only went into the ground, but also rose up out of it in many places. As he looked even closer, he realized that all the trees were connected by a single root system. He then slowly began to understand that the root system extended throughout the entire planet, to all trees in all forests—a wonderful image of the interconnectedness of all life.

I have already mentioned that animal images of the Self appear at key moments of transformation in our lives. Two such moments occur when we have 1) integrated the Shadow and go on to deal with the Anima/Animus; and 2) later when we have integrated the syzygy and must now deal directly with the Self.

At each point, we are likely to have dreams where the moment of transition is mirrored by an overt transformation in our dreams, and some image of the Self is likely to be present in those dreams. For example, at the point of integrating the Shadow, a patient dreamed of watching someone wading at the beach. Suddenly another man— whom the dreamer thought of as "the spy" (the Shadow)—ran toward the wading man, grabbed him and pulled him under the water. A minute later, the wading man came up alone, but the dreamer knew it was really the spy. At that moment of realization, he and the wading man and the spy became one. He then found himself swimming in a huge swimming pool, with a lovely woman (the Anima). Off at the side looking on was her grandfather, a wise and powerful man (the Self).

In a dream of integrating the Anima, a man dreamed of a tiny man and woman (the Anima), only inches high— which seemed normal in the dream. A large monitor lizard (the Self), several feet long, came into the room. The man stood apart, wary but unafraid. The woman panicked, ran, then fell on the floor. The lizard came over to her, then melted into a cloud and went inside her through her mouth. In a moment, she seemed to transform from the inside out, until there was a lizard once more, though one that looked somewhat different than before. The man was too far away to come to the woman's aid, and watched with some sense of detachment.

These dreams of transformation sound frightening to waking consciousness, but possess a sense of rightness during the dream—another sure sign of the presence of the Self.

THE MANA PERSONALITY

> . . . a mana-personality [is] a being full of some occult and bewitching quality (*mana*), endowed with magical knowledge and power.[15]

Once the Anima/Animus has been integrated into the personality, a transitional figure appears, who prefigures the Self, and, in fact, is an inferior version of the Self. Jung termed it alternately the "Mana-personality" and the "Magician."

Melanesians use the word *mana* to denote an impersonal, supernatural force possessed by people or objects. Anthropologists quickly realized what a wonderful general term it was, and came to use mana to describe a wide variety of similar beliefs among traditional cultures. Jung in turn appropriated it from the anthropologists. Both Jung and the anthropologists would undoubtedly agree that mana lies in the mind of the beholder, not in the object itself. However, I think that most anthropologists

---

[15]Carl Jung, *Collected Works*, Vol. 7, 375.

would consider mana as a cultural derivative; i.e., some person or thing only possesses mana because the people in the culture agree that it does. In contrast, Jung argues that a person or object possesses mana because it represents an archetype; over their incredibly long history, the archetypes accumulate mana unto themselves.

In chapter 2, we discussed how Jung came to his discovery of complexes in the psyche. As you will recall, he found that when he stripped away the emotionally charged personal associations that grouped together in a complex (such as a mother or father complex, for example), instead of defusing the energy, he arrived at an impersonal, archetypal core which was even more emotionally charged. Initially Jung used the word *libido* (Freud's term for sexual energy) for this energy, but libido for Jung was not limited to sexual energy. Later he used the word *mana* to represent this impersonal energy; more often he just called it energy. I will use both mana and energy in the rest of this book.

The key realization is that archetypes possess mana, and that this mana has nothing to do with personal emotional connections to the archetype. The deeper we go into the collective unconscious, the greater the mana. When we start the process of individuation and encounter the Shadow, we have to struggle not only with personal issues, but with the collective archetype of the feared "other" which lies behind our personal fears.

As we deal with the Shadow, we come to realize that our anger and disgust is really at ourselves. As the blindfold of our own projections falls from our eyes, we find that we possess hopes and desires, abilities and possibilities, not contained within our original self-image. That self-image now feels cramped. But, though the Shadow is a collective figure known to all cultures, we are not yet deep into the collective unconscious. In dealing with the

Shadow, most of our struggle is with our personal unconscious.

With the Anima/Animus, we are dealing largely with collective experience, though, initially we deal with the Shadow aspect of the Anima/Animus, which is still largely a struggle with the personal unconscious. Then, even when we come to the archetypal aspect of the Anima/Animus, much of the time we deal with personal difficulties with relationships. But the real power of the Anima/Animus comes from the collective experience of humanity in dealing with the problem of relationship, especially the relationship between a man and a woman.

Our struggles with the Anima/Animus syzygy are so much more difficult than those with the Shadow because the syzygy is one step deeper into the collective unconscious. Accordingly, the Anima/Animus has much more energy than the Shadow. The Self is still further from consciousness, and hence, is still more difficult to consciously acknowledge as part of our individual psyches – and possesses still more energy.

With the Shadow, we say, "that's not me," and curl our lips with repugnance. With the Anima/Animus, we say, "that's not me," but we are likely to be interested (though perhaps also fearful). With the Self, we say, "that's not me," and bow our heads, or run in fear. The Self seems definitely beyond human realization. But nevertheless it is also a part of us; without it we would be something less than fully human.

Those who are brave enough and lucky enough to integrate the Anima/Animus "swallow" a lot of collective energy they are not entitled to, and eventually find it to be highly indigestible. When they first try to digest it, they puff up and think they have become the holder of secret knowledge far beyond the ken of normal men and women. In Jungian terms, they become "inflated," filled with mana that doesn't belong to them.

People who consciously walk the path of individuation had better learn to recognize when they are becoming inflated. People who bring the numinous figures of the unconscious into consciousness by way of dream interpretation, active imagination, etc., will invariably alternate between fits of inflation and depression. It can no more be avoided that we can avoid getting wet when we step into the ocean. We have to recognize when we are getting too full of ourselves, and then consciously dampen the inflation; or, recognize the depression as equally inhuman and reconnect with the world.

The important realization is that the more than human energy we are feeling is not ours—it belongs to the collective history of mankind and is contained within the archetypes. As long as we are gripped by an archetype, we are literally inhuman, merely flat figures designed by the centuries to fit all time and all situations. Caught within that grip, there is no development, no change.

Unfortunately, many people never get past the stage of the mana-personality. They take on the mantle of the magician or the witch, the guru or sage, the wise man or the sorceress. Or else they project the image out onto someone else, and take on the equally shallow role of the master's disciple. Neither role is likely to lead to a promising outcome. These twin outcomes are especially likely in spiritual traditions that don't deal progressively with the Shadow and the Anima/Animus, but try to advance directly toward some ultimate value—the Light, Nirvana, oneness with God, etc.

The struggles with the Shadow and the syzygy help develop psychic and moral muscles, which help in dealing with the mana-personality. People who have integrated the Shadow will never forget just how deluded we can be about our thoughts and desires. People who have integrated the Anima/Animus will never forget just how deluded we can be about feelings and values. The humility that develops from such experiences is a powerful armor against inflation.

SELF-ACTUALIZATION

Once past the delusion that we are the mana-personality, we are forced to ask ourselves who we actually are. More than at any other stage of the individuation process, the question of self-definition becomes paramount now. We are now continually exposed to a portion of ourselves that is the best we can ever be. It, in fact, contains possibilities that exceed our human limitations. How can we reconcile the person we are with the person we could be?

Time after time, alternate temptations toward inflation and depression appear. How is it possible to contain wholeness within the human psyche? How can we balance extremes of thought and feeling, spirit and instinct? Humanistic psychologist Abraham Maslow provided insight into this question with his concept of self-actualization. Maslow felt that psychologists spent too much time studying dysfunctional people. Maslow began studying people who routinely functioned at a higher level than the average. In surveys, he asked people to pick historical figures who were considered exceptional models of what a human being should be, and asked them to describe why they picked these people.

In compiling these surveys, he found there was wide agreement on a significant number of people—people such as Beethoven, Thoreau, Abraham Lincoln, Albert Einstein. Though each was a strongly individual personality, Maslow found that a small number of words were mentioned repeatedly in describing them, both by the people he surveyed and in biographies—words such as whole, complete, just, alive, simple, beautiful, truthful, etc. And one essential feature stood out among all these figures: both their motivations and their rewards seemed to come largely from within (from the Self in Jung's terms). Accordingly, Maslow chose the apt term *self-actualized* to describe them.

To these historical figures, Maslow added a number of people he knew well enough to consider as worthy of inclusion. Though none of them may have been an Abraham Lincoln or an Albert Einstein, they had one distinct advantage for Maslow: he could give them a variety of psychological tests to objectively test their character traits. Again the same traits emerged, again their motivations came from within, not from some external value system. When asked about their deepest values, they used words like justice, or beauty, or truth, etc. But when Maslow probed deeper into what they meant by "justice," for example, he found that justice for them meant truthful, and beautiful, and whole, etc. Similarly, someone whose highest value was truth, considered truth to be just and beautiful, etc. At the deepest level, they all had the same values; they merely picked one aspect of that deepest value which reflected their individual personality.

With a well-defined picture of the characteristics of self-actualized men and women, Maslow then turned his studies toward normal people in their best moments, moments he termed "peak-experiences." Once again, when describing how they acted and felt during those moments, the words picked were wholeness, beauty, truth, etc.

Maslow felt that he had demonstrated that humanity at its best is self-actualized, rather than motivated by external values and rewards. Further, self-actualized people, though wildly different in personality, were more alike than not in their basic approach to life and in the values they cherished. Normal people, who may not normally reach the heights of such self-actualized people, are also capable of exhibiting similar characteristics in their best moments.

Maslow's ideas had an enormous influence on psychology in the 1960s. Although he wasn't alone in reacting against the prevailing behavioral school of psychology that dominated American psychology at the time, he was the major influence in the creation of humanistic psychology (and later transpersonal psychology). As we discussed in chapter 2 in our description of Marshall McLuhan's ideas, it can be a curse to become too popular too quickly. Today Maslow has fallen into disfavor (though not so completely as McLuhan), and his work isn't much talked about. For many, he remains a nearly forgotten part of the 60s, like LSD and student riots.

Maslow's conclusions are no less important today than when he was in vogue. And they fit closely with Jung's concepts of the individuation process, and the relationship between the ego and the Self. Perhaps Maslow overemphasized the light and forgot the dark, perhaps he failed to sufficiently appreciate the difficulties of self-actualization. Beethoven, Thoreau, Lincoln, and Einstein, for example, were all subject to intense feelings of depression throughout their lives. Such experience is common for those who travel far down the path of individuation, because they find that there is always more darkness to face.

But, regardless of the darkness they are forced to confront, Maslow found that self-actualized people remain healthier, and are able to cope with tragedies that would crush lesser people. As a group they feel more deeply, grieve more fully, but are then able to leave their grief behind and get on with life. They are people who accomplish things despite seemingly insurmountable obstacles. Unfortunately, Maslow failed to realize that the wholeness which drew him to self-actualized people had its source in the darkness. This overemphasis on the light leaves

Maslow's work in danger of presenting a Pollyanna view of reality. But, nevertheless, he provided a great service by reminding us of the possibilities we all possess.[16]

CREATIVITY AND THE SELF

. . . we stand with our soul suspended between formidable influences from within and from without, and somehow we must be fair to both. This we can do only after the measure of our individual capacities. Hence we must bethink ourselves not so much of what we "ought" to do as of what we *can* and *must* do.[17]

There is no way to sum up the Self, nor to adequately describe all the challenges life presents once one has developed a conscious relationship with the Self. Though the path of individuation has been presented in this book through the three separate stages of Shadow, Anima/Animus, and Self, there is only one continuous process— the relationship between consciousness and the Self. Our struggle with the Shadow is, after all, an attempt at transcendence and wholeness, albeit at a lower level. We can't begin to be one with our total reality unless we first face who we are and what we desire.

The Anima/Animus stage is again a search for wholeness. How can we be whole until we are willing to be torn between the moral choices that confront anyone who lives fully?

When the Self begins to make its appearance in our lives, there are often unusual side effects. For example, it

---

[16]See Abraham Maslow, *Toward a Psychology of Being* (New York: Van Nostrand Reinhold, 1968), and *Religion, Values and Peak Experiences* (New York: Penguin Books, 1976) for details on his studies and theories.

[17]Carl Jung, *Collected Works*, Vol. 7, 397.

isn't uncommon to have wide swings of emotion: not only the swings between inflation and depression that we have already mentioned as central, but also bursts of anger or tears seemingly coming from nowhere. Often some fairly extreme physical reaction occurs—a bout of the flu, intense muscle aches and pains, nausea. Parapsychological phenomena are also common—ranging from hunches which are almost always right to precognitive dreams. Some people will be strongly attracted by the almost physical nature of the energy the Self produces. In addition, ego inflation will cause many to fall into the trap of becoming some sort of guru when the Self appears.[18]

All this is a consequence of the extremes of the energy, the mana, produced when a channel is opened to the collective unconscious through the Self. As we discussed with the mana-personality, some way has to be found to release that energy before we are tempted to claim it as our own, or be possessed by it and become its pawn. Humility is a necessary starting point, but not sufficient in itself. Once begun, there is no way to cut off the energy generated by the pathway to the collective unconscious provided by the Self. Instead we have to find some way to use that energy *creatively*.

The forms which that creativity can take are as varied as the people involved, but any form of creativity is, in essence, a translation of darkness into light. Everything new originates in the collective unconscious. However, it is not enough for us to serve as simple conduits, despite how popular "channeling" is today. Though the new

---

[18]All these reactions have been described in many traditions which have explicit paths for spiritual development—Hindu, Buddhist, Native American, etc. They are viewed as transitional phenomena. For a detailed description of these reactions within the Hindu tradition of Kundalini energy, see Gopi Krishna's account of his own experience in *Kundalini: The Evolutionary Energy in Man* (Boston: Shambhala Publications, 1967).

invariably comes from the unconscious, it is consciousness that gives the new explicit form. Cut off from the unconscious, consciousness is bleak and unvarying. But, given free rein, the unconscious trots out the same unchanging symbols it has used through the millennia. It is in the relationship between consciousness and the unconscious that something truly new and creative emerges.

Engaged consciously in that relationship, life becomes an adventure, filled with challenge. By this stage in the individuation process there is no turning back. And the challenge is always essentially the same—just when we have achieved some degree of wholeness in our lives, the unconscious presents us with a new challenge that totally disrupts our view of reality. And since new experience is intolerable, we are forced to make sense out of the strange new world that confronts us. In psychologist Rollo May's words:

> . . . You can live without a father who accepts you, but you cannot live without a world that makes sense to you.[19]

We have to engage with the new challenge, and slowly integrate it into our lives in a creative fashion. Each time, the unconscious presents us with more new data than consciousness can understand or accept. Then, once that new data has been integrated into our own lives, it has to be creatively shared with others. Most often, the integration process, itself, is best achieved by attempting to create something new for others.

If there were no collective unconscious, the unconscious would contain nothing but personal memories and desires which we had overlooked or repressed. It might require courage to face some of those memories and

---

[19]Rollo May, *The Courage to Create* ((New York: W. W. Norton & Company, 1975), p. 133.

desires, but all would have passed through our consciousness at some point and would be capable of being integrated. But if there is a collective unconscious—and this whole book has been an attempt to present the reasons why Jung considered it to exist—the situation is much different.

Archetypal material has little or nothing to do with our personal lives. It has enormous mana because it has been stored away over millennia through the progressive evolution of not only humanity, but through the entire evolutionary history of life itself. When such unconscious material confronts consciousness, we are presented with the following dilemma: 1) the energy it possesses is so strong that we need desperately to find a way to contain it; yet 2) we have no ready containers available in consciousness; it won't fit into our existing value system. Since we are being confronted by material from the collective unconscious, we have no conscious resources immediately available to structure the material.

That's the challenge of the individuation process. Somehow we have to discover some personal connection to the archetypal images, feelings and behaviors. Gradually we have to separate out what can be related to the personal life from that which belongs to the ages. Though the process can be inordinately difficult, it can also be lavishly rewarding. Life gains a purpose which, because it comes from within, can never be exhausted.

The essential realizations we gain from each stage of the individuation process are simple—in retrospect. But unless we struggle through each stage ourselves, those realizations are nothing more than homilies; it is the struggle that gives each its individual resonance. Remember that the world is very, very old, and consciousness is very, very new. Consciousness is still far from able to provide an adequate lens to view all of reality.

From the Shadow stage we learn that the despised "other" is really us. Once we realize that we are essentially looking into a microscope and seeing ourselves staring back, it becomes less necessary to denigrate differences. Those differences all become future possibilities. But, having separated ourselves from the world, in order to isolate that part of the world which is really ours, it then becomes time to discover what the rest of the world is really like.

From the Anima/Animus stage, we learn that we are not alone, that our entire life is a relationship. At any moment in our lives, we are connected in relationships that connect with other relationships, eventually touching every person, every animal, every mountain, every stream. The wonderful paradox is that each person is the center of this amazing web of relationships. Having realized that it is impossible to be truly separate from the world, we need to find how we can contain that more than human wholeness within us.

Finally, from the Self, we learn that the wholeness we seek is our essential nature. The alienation we so often feel, the inner split that gives us so much grief, is created by consciousness out of fear and ignorance. Consciousness is still immature and thinks that it should be able to contain everything in tidy little compartments. When it can't, it grows afraid and builds ever more permanent walls between those categories. Sometimes, it grows so fearful that it walls itself up in one and won't come out.

> Sensing the self as something irrational, as an indefinable existent, to which the ego is neither opposed nor subjected, but merely attached, and about which it revolves much as the earth revolves around the sun—thus we come to the goal of individuation.[20]

---

[20]Carl Jung, *Collected Works*, Vol. 7, 405.

Man does not change at death into his immortal part, but is mortal and immortal even in life, being both ego and Self.[21]

Gradually, as our fear of the "god within us" dies, as our arrogant usurpation of its powers and insights passes away, it becomes a mirror for both who we are at any given time—and who we can be. At first, the distance between the two seems daunting. But gradually we come to see that the problem isn't the distance between our actuality and our possibilities, because there is some greater part of us that can contain both.

---

[21]Carl Jung, *Collected Works*, Vol. 5, 384, fn 182.

AFTERWORD

Any attempt to summarize all of Jung's works would necessarily be either very long or very sketchy. In writing this introduction to Jung's psychology, I have had to make many difficult choices about what to include and what to leave out. Without doubt, the central idea in Jungian psychology is the existence of the collective unconscious and our relationship to it through the individuation process, and I have chosen to structure this introductory volume around the individuation process. In doing so, I have given some background into Jung's life so that the reader can see how he came to such startling conclusions.

One of my own initial attractions to Jung's psychology was that it accomplished the remarkable feat of bridging the gap between the spiritual and scientific worlds. I have tried to capture both sides in this book (including providing a fair amount of scientific support for Jung's worldview that wasn't available in Jung's time). But in order to keep this book as short as it is, I have had to curtail both to the point where only a flavor of Jung's own twin interests remains.

In the scientific realm, in particular, I have had to ignore Jung's joint discovery with physicist Wolfgang Pauli of the *psychoid* nature of reality,[1] which is that a unitary world underlies both the deepest archetypal level of the psyche and the deepest quantum level of matter. One

---

[1]Carl Jung; Wolfgang Pauli, *The Interpretation of Nature and the Psyche* (New York: Bollingen Series, Pantheon Books, 1955).

of Jung's most significant and influential concepts — *synchronicity* — came out of that discovery. In brief, synchronicity is the concept that there are acausal connections between people, places, and things in the world.[2] Synchronicity (albeit under other names) is becoming more widely accepted in contemporary science largely because of the widespread experimental support for Bell's Theorem in physics. Bell's Theorem indicates that subatomic particles remain connected in some acausal fashion, even when widely separated in space.

Synchronicity and the psychoid nature of reality also connect closely with Jung's hypothesis that numbers are the most primitive archetype of order, and thus form the bridge between the outer and inner worlds. Jung's colleague Marie-Louise von Franz has extended this work in her book *Number and Time*.[3] This area is a particular favorite of mine.

I have barely touched on Jung's detailed elaboration of key archetypes such as the Child, the Father, the Mother, the Trickster, the Hero, etc. Jungian psychologists have written extensively about these and other archetypes.

The single most important aspect of Jung's psychology, which I have had to suppress in this book, is his use of alchemy as a model for the individuation process. Unfortunately, this area is quite complex. Both Marie-Louise von Franz and Edward Edinger have extended Jung's work in this area, but to date no one has provided an introduction to this very valuable material for a general public.

There are many significant books about Jung's psychology; however, I strongly encourage the reader to read Jung directly. Jung has an undeserved reputation for being

---

[2]Acausal simply means *not* attributable to physical cause-and-effect.
[3]Marie-Louise von Franz, *Number and Time* (Evanston, IL: Northwestern University Press, 1974).

difficult to read. Using this book as a roadmap to the structure and dynamics of the collective unconscious, the reader can feel free to dive into any of Jung's collected works, all of which are available in quality paperbound editions. There are also many quality paperbound collections of Jung's material on specific topics, such as dreams, key archetypes, etc. Probably the best introduction to Jung's own writing is through his spiritual autobiography, *Memories, Dreams, Reflections*.[4] I hope that this book has opened your eyes to a very different view of reality, and at least whetted your appetite to explore Jung's psychology and your own process of individuation.

---

[4]Carl Jung, *Memories, Dreams, Reflections* (New York: Pantheon Books, revised edition, 1973).

REFERENCES

Bennet, E. A. 1985. *Meetings with Jung*. Zürich: Daimon Verlag.
English psychotherapist E. A. Bennet was a long-time friend of Jung's. This book contains Bennet's journal entries recording his conversations with Jung during the last fifteen years of Jung's life.

BMB. March 29, 1982. Los Angeles: Brain/Mind Bulletin.
Describes psychiatrist William Gray's extension of Paul McLean's triune brain theory.

Bro, Harmon H. 1985. *Dreams in the Life of Prayer & Meditation: The Approach of Edgar Cayce*. Virginia Beach, VA: Inner Vision.
Full of practical material summarizing Edgar Cayce's approach to dream work, much of which fits well with Jungian dream work.

Campbell, Joseph. 1990. *The Hero with a Thousand Faces* (rev. ed.). Princeton: Bollingen Series: No. XVII. Princeton University Press.
Single best portrait of the individuation process, pictured through the stages of the "hero's journey." Interested readers can also find this revised edition in paperback.

_____. (ed.). 1971. *The Portable Jung*. New York: Penguin Books.
Best one-volume selection of Jung's writings. Contains a valuable chronology of the major events in Jung's life.

Donn, Linda. 1988. *Freud and Jung: Years of Friendship, Years of Loss.* New York: Charles Scribner's Sons.
> The best and most reliable portrait of the relationship between Freud and Jung.

Edinger, Edward F. *Ego and Archetype.* 1972. Baltimore: Penguin Books.
> One of the few truly great Jungian books by other than Jung. It follows the individuation process through observing the dynamics of the relationship between the ego and the Self.

Ferguson, Marilyn. 1973. *The Brain Revolution.* New York: Taplinger Publishing Company.
> Contains the wonderful anecdote about state-dependent memory in a Charlie Chaplin film.

Ferguson, Marilyn; Coleman, Wim; Perrin, Pat. 1990. *PragMagic.* New York: Pocket Books.
> Includes sections summarizing much recent work on sleep and dreams, and memory.

Freuchen, Peter. 1961. *Book of the Eskimos.* Cleveland, OH: The World Publishing Company.
> A totally fascinating portrait of the Eskimos by a sympathetic European who grew to know them, and love them, in the period when their culture was just beginning to be overrun by the West.

Gardner, Howard. 1985. *The Mind's New Science.* New York: Basic Books.
> A wonderful synthesis of a wide variety of ongoing scientific discoveries, which have come to be grouped under the general term, cognitive science.

Grant, John. 1984. *Dreamers: A Geography of Dreamland.* London: Grafton Books.
> More useful for its extensive compilation of dreams by categories than for its analysis of dreams.

Hannah, Barbara. 1976. *Jung: His Life and Work.* New York: Capricorn Books, G. P. Putnam's Sons.

A moving portrait of Jung's life from one of his closest disciples.

Hartmann, Ernest. 1988. "Sleep." In Armand M. Nicholi, Jr., M.D. (ed.). *The New Harvard Guide to Psychiatry*. New York: Beknap Press.
Contains some updating of research on sleep and dreams.

Humphrey, Nicholas. 1984. *Consciousness Regained*. Oxford: Oxford University Press.
Humphrey's theory of the purpose of dreams is discussed in chapter 3.

Jacobi, Jolande; Hull, R.F.C. (eds.). 1973. *C. G. Jung: Psychological Reflections*. Princeton: Bollingen Series, Princeton University Press.
Exceptional collection of short excerpts from Jung's collected works, arranged by topic.

Jaffe, Aniela. 1984. *Jung's Last Years* (revised ed.). Dallas, TX: Spring Publications.
Aniela Jaffe was Jung's private secretary and companion in his last years. We get a portrait of genius still flourishing in his last years, but also of a Jung irritable and seemingly not at peace with himself.

Jenks, Kathleen. 1975. *Journey of a Dream Animal*. New York: Julian Press.
A unique book, which records a woman's "human search for personal identity" through her dreams. Because she went through this process alone, rather than in analysis, her insights are hard-won and personal. I can't imagine anyone working with dreams who couldn't learn a great deal from this book.

Jung, C. G. *Collected Works* (20 volumes). Princeton: Bollingen Series, Princeton University Press.

_____. 1933. *Modern Man in Search of his Soul*. New York: Harvest.
A moving introduction to Jung's ideas through a personal selection of his essays.

———. 1958. *The Undiscovered Self.* New York: Mentor Books, New American Library.

A wonderful introduction to Jung for the layperson, probably second only to *Modern Man in Search of a Soul*.

———. 1968. *Analytical Psychology: Its Theory and Practice.* New York: Vintage Books.

Contains the lectures given at the Tavistock Clinic in 1935. Probably the best summation of Jung's theories, prior to his discovery of the alchemical model of the psyche.

———. 1973. *Memories, Dreams, Reflections* (revised ed.). New York: Pantheon Books.

A unique book: an autobiography of Jung's spiritual progress.

———. 1984. *Dream Analysis: Notes of the Seminar given in 1928–1930.* Princeton: Bollingen Series, Princeton University Press.

Another valuable source of information on Jungian dream analysis.

Jung, C. G.; Pauli, W. 1955. *The Interpretation of Nature and the Psyche.* New York: Bollingen Series, Pantheon Books.

Contains both Jung's seminal work "Synchronicity: An Acausal Connecting Principle" and Pauli's "The Influence of Archetypal Ideas on the Scientific Theories of Kepler."

Krishna, Gopi. 1967. *Kundalini: The Evolutionary Energy in Man.* Boston: Shambhala Publications.

A personal account of the frightening power released inside Gopi Krishna by the Kundalini energy.

Kronenberger, Louis. (ed.). 1947. *The Portable Johnson & Boswell.* New York: Viking Press.

Contains excerpts from Boswell's *Life of Johnson*,

including Johnson's supposed refutation of Bishop Berkeley.

LaBerge, Stephen, Ph.D. 1985. *Lucid Dreaming*. New York: Ballantine Books.
The first book on lucid dreaming, by a pioneer of research in the subject.

Laszlo, Violet S. de. 1958. *Psyche and Symbol*. Garden City: Doubleday Anchor Books.
An excellent one-volume selection of Jung's writings which complements Campbell's selection in *The Portable Jung*.

Lorenz, Konrad. 1952. *King Solomon's Ring*. New York: Crowell.
Delightful book. Contains the story and pictures of Lorenz's baby goose who "imprinted" the mother archetype onto Lorenz.

Loye, David. 1983. *The Sphinx and the Rainbow*. New York: Bantam.
A masterful popular portrait of virtually everything known about the brain.

Luce, Gay Gaer; Segal, Julius. 1967. *Sleep*. New York: Lancer Books.
Though two decades old, still the best single volume on most of the major dream research. About the only area not covered is the more recent research in lucid dreaming.

Marchand, Philip. 1989. *Marshall McLuhan: The Medium and the Messenger*. New York: Ticknor & Fields.
An extremely readable biography, which captures both the prophet and the charlatan in McLuhan.

Maslow, Abraham. 1968. *Toward a Psychology of Being*. New York: Van Nostrand Reinhold.
Maslow's single most significant book. It records most of his key ideas about self-actualization.

———. 1976. *Religion, Values and Peak-Experiences*. New York: Penguin Books.
Maslow's studies of peak and nadir experiences.

May, Rollo. 1975. *The Courage to Create*. New York: W. W. Norton & Company.
Like Jung, Rollo May views creativity as the ultimate challenge of the individuation process.

McLuhan, Marshall. 1962. *The Gutenberg Galaxy: The Making of Typographic Man*. Toronto: University of Toronto Press.
McLuhan's breakthrough book, which first presented his theory that the invention of moveable type led to a change in human consciousness.

———. 1964. *Understanding Media: The Extensions of Man*. New York: Signet Books.
McLuhan's most important book. Like all of McLuhan's work, its almost total lack of any normal organization makes it both delightful and frustrating to read.

Metzner, Ralph. 1979. *Know Your Type*. New York: Anchor.
Extremely thorough compilation of virtually every important typological system ever devised.

Otto, Rudolf. 1950. *The Idea of the Holy*. London: Oxford University Press. Paperback reprint, 1958.
Otto's most famous work, in which he first mentions the concept of a "numinous" aspect of reality.

Pribram, Karl. 1981. "The Brain." In Alberto Villoldo and Ken Dychtwald (eds.). *Millennium: Glimpses into the 21st Century*. Los Angeles: J. P. Tarcher.
Pribram's own account of the research that led him to his discovery of the holographic brain model.

Reed, Henry. (ed.). 1977–1979. *Sundance Community Dream Journal*. Virginia Beach, VA: A.R.E. Press.
One of the most fascinating journals of all time: a record of an ongoing community experiment in dream research along lines suggested by Edgar

Cayce. Dr. Henry Reed organized this work and developed many unique dream techniques.

_____. 1985. *Getting Help from your Dreams*. Virginia Beach, VA: Inner Vision.
One of the true pioneers of *meaningful* dream research shares many of his techniques for using dreams to help live your life more meaningfully.

Reese, W. L. 1980. *Dictionary of Philosophy and Religion*. Atlantic Highlands, NJ: Humanities Press.
Mammoth, highly readable one-volume encyclopedia of philosophy. Useful as short reference source for many concepts presented in this book.

Robertson, Robin. 1987. *C. G. Jung and the Archetypes of the Collective Unconscious*. New York: Peter Lang.
Traces the history of the concept of archetypes of the collective unconscious, first in philosophy leading to Jung's psychology, then in mathematics leading to Kurt Gödel's proof that mathematics is necessarily incomplete.

_____. 1990. *After the End of Time: Revelation and the Growth of Consciousness*. Virginia Beach, VA: Inner Vision.
Looks at the Book of Revelation in the Bible as if it were a big dream about a transition in consciousness. Develops many themes just touched on in this book.

Rose, Steven. 1976. *The Conscious Brain*. New York: Vintage Books.
Especially good in pointing out the need to transcend a brain/mind dualism.

Rosenfield, Israel. 1988. *The Invention of Memory*. New York: Basic Books.
Presents Nobel Prize-winning immunologist Gerald Edelman's theory of "neural Darwinism." This theory presents memory as a creative activity.

Rossi, Ernest Lawrence. 1980. "As Above, So Below: The Holographic Mind." *Psychological Perspectives,* Fall 1990.

    Describes Pribram's theory of the holographic mind and relates it both to mysticism and to Jung's psychology.

_____. 1985. *Dreams and the Growth of Personality.* New York: Brunner/Mazel.

    Combines the latest research on dreams with practical experience with a single patient from a Jungian viewpoint. Filled with insights into the dream process. Highly recommended.

_____. 1986. *The Psychobiology of Mind-Body Healing.* New York: W. W. Norton & Company.

    Contains chapter on state-dependent learning and memory.

Russell, Peter. 1979. *The Brain Book.* New York: Hawthorn Books.

    An excellent popular summary of recent knowledge about the brain.

Russo, Richard A. (ed.). 1987. *Dreams are Wiser than Men.* Berkeley: North Atlantic Books.

    A wonderful collection of essays, poems and anecdotes about dreams.

Sagan, Carl. 1977. *The Dragons of Eden: Speculations of the Evolution of Human Intelligence.* New York: Ballantine Books.

    Describes scientist Paul MacLean's triune brain model.

Sanford, John A. 1991. *Soul Journey: A Jungian Analyst Looks at Reincarnation.* New York: Crossroad Publishing Company.

    The best scholarly book written on reincarnation. Contains a wonderful history of the religious concept of the soul.

Sharp, Daryl. 1991. *Jung Lexicon: A Primer of Terms & Concepts*. Toronto: Inner City Books.
Useful for those new to Jung, especially as the definitions are fleshed-out with quotes from Jung.

Sheldrake, Rupert. 1981. *A New Science of Life: The Hypothesis of Formative Causation*. Los Angeles: J. P. Tarcher.
Uses data from behavioral psychology to support concept of morphogenetic fields, which closely correspond to Jung's archetypes.

_____. 1987. "Mind, Memory and Archetype." In *Psychological Perspectives*, Spring 1987. Los Angeles: C. G. Jung Institute.
Discusses concept that memory is not localized in the brain.

Snow, C. P. 1968. *The Sleep of Reason*. New York: Charles Scribner's Sons.
One of the novels in Snow's eleven-volume "Strangers and Brothers" series. It discusses the trial of two women who cold-bloodedly tortured a little boy.

Stern, Paul J. 1976. *C. G. Jung: The Haunted Prophet*. New York: George Braziller.
Hostile biography of Jung. Should be read with caution.

Stillinger, Jack. (ed.). 1965. *William Wordsworth: Selected Poems and Prefaces*. Boston: Houghton Mifflin Company.
In addition to "Tintern Abbey," which is quoted in this book, readers should examine Wordsworth's epic masterpiece "The Prelude."

Storr, Anthony. 1983. *The Essential Jung*. Princeton, NJ: Princeton University Press.
A newer one-volume compilation of excerpts from Jung's writings, which some prefer to Campbell's groundbreaking *The Portable Jung*.

Vallant, George E. 1977. *Adaption to Life: How the Best and the Brightest Came of Age*. Boston: Little, Brown & Company.

A well-written, wise summary of the results of the Grant Study.

von Franz, Marie-Louise. 1974. *Number and Time*. Evanston, IL: Northwestern University Press.

Develops Jung's late hypothesis that number is the most primitive archetype of order.

——. 1975. *C. G. Jung: His Myth in Our Time*. New York: C. G. Jung Foundation for Analytical Psychology, G. P. Putnam's Son.

A biography both of Jung's life and psychic development; as such, is an ideal companion work to Jung's own *Memories, Dreams, Reflections*.

von Franz, Marie-Louise; Hillman, James. 1971. *Jung's Typology*. Dallas, TX: Spring Publications.

A treasure-house of information on Jung's theory of psychological types. Contains both von Franz's "The Inferior Function," and Hillman's "The Feeling Function."

Watson, Peter. 1982. *Twins: An Uncanny Relationship?* New York: Viking Press.

Watson's stories of the correspondences in the lives of identical twins, separated early in life, provides strong corroboration for Jung's concept of the archetypal basis of the individuation process.

Wehr, Gerhard. 1987. *Jung: A Biography*. Boston: Shambhala Publications.

Massive, clumsily written biography of Jung, but contains much useful background material presented nowhere else.

Whitmont, Edward C. 1969. *The Symbolic Quest*. Princeton, NJ: Princeton University Press.

The standard introduction to Jung's thought, written at a more technical level than the book you are reading.

Wilhelm, Richard. (trans.) 1962. *The Secret of the Golden Flower.* New York: Harvest.

Translation of an ancient Chinese alchemical text. Contains a foreword and a commentary by Jung, in which he explains how this was the first book which led him to understand the alchemical underpinning of the psyche.

INDEX

Robin Robertson has a B.S. in Mathematics and a B.A. in English Literature from the University of Maryland. He went on to earn an M.A. in Counselling Psychology and a Ph.D. in Clinical Psychology, and is the author of two other books about Jungian psychology. From 1986 to 1990, he served as staff editor and wrote book reviews for *Psychological Perspectives*, a Jungian journal. This book is the result of a longtime fascination with the "real magic" underlying our day-to-day reality—a topic of significance to the many people who are curious about exploring the psyche and pursuing the process of conscious living.